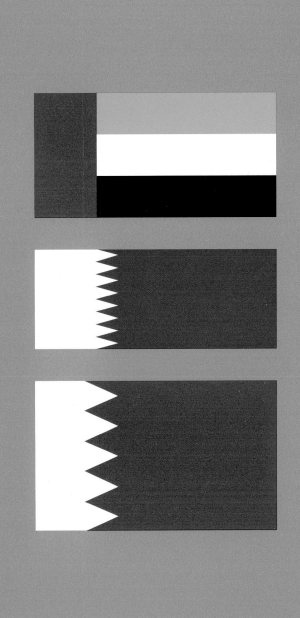

AE

PHILIP JODIDIO

ARCHITECTURE IN THE EMIRATES

TASCHEN

HONG KONG KÖLN LONDON LOS ANGELES MADRID PARIS TOKYO

#4

7/10/12 #
16/18/18

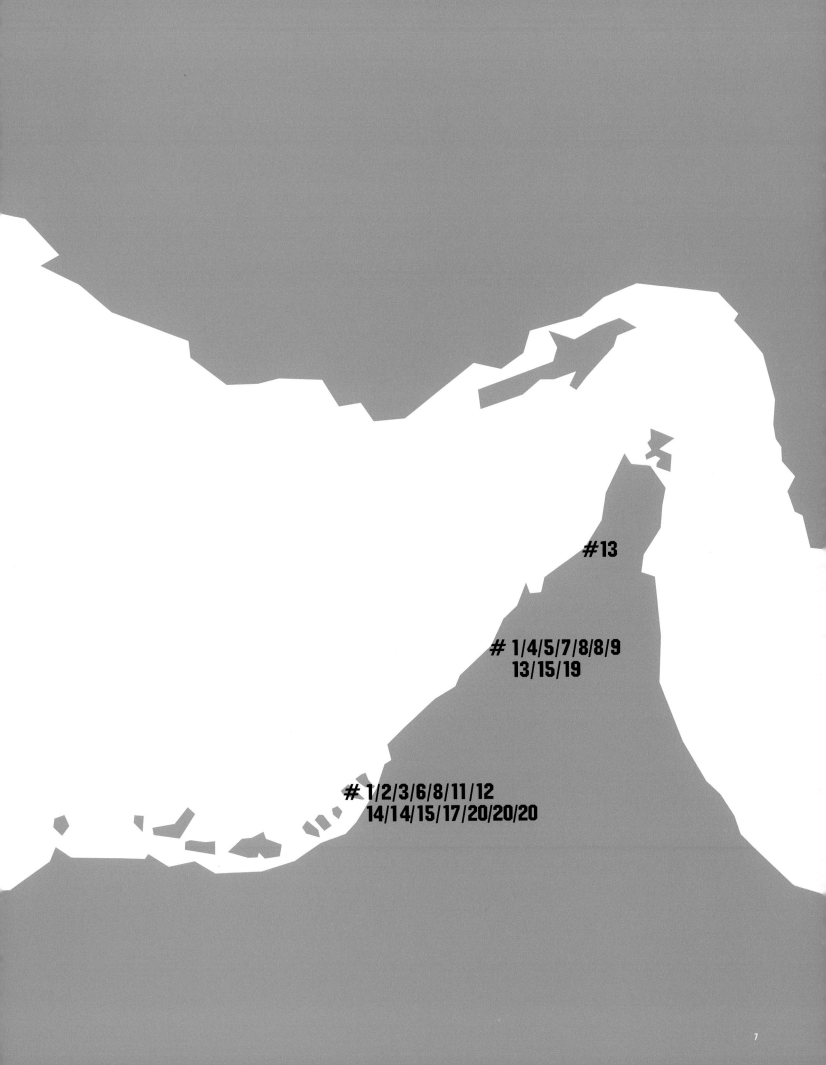

#13

1/4/5/7/8/8/9
13/15/19

1/2/3/6/8/11/12
14/14/15/17/20/20/20

INTRODUCTION

THE EMERALD CITY

"Even with eyes protected by the green spectacles, Dorothy and her friends were at first dazzled by the brilliancy of the wonderful City. The streets were lined with beautiful houses all built of green marble and studded everywhere with sparkling emeralds. They walked over a pavement of the same green marble, and where the blocks were joined together were rows of emeralds, set closely, and glittering in the brightness of the sun. The window panes were of green glass; even the sky above the City had a green tint, and the rays of the sun were green."

L. Frank Baum, *The Wonderful Wizard of Oz[1]*

Few areas of the world can match the sheer economic upsurge of the Gulf Emirates. In certain Gulf cities, most recently Dubai, Abu Dhabi or Doha, a remarkable construction fever has taken hold, with towers rising in all directions. Ambitious construction is not entirely new to the region. Indeed, when he created the Aga Khan Award for Architecture in the late 1970s, the leader of the world's Ismaili Muslims was seeking in part to offer a counterpoint to what he saw as a headlong rush to build the culturally disconnected architecture seen at the time in Kuwait and elsewhere. It can be said of most modern cities, even such Western centers as New York, that quality architecture is more the exception than the rule; certainly, the vertiginous development of the Gulf Emirates in the past few years has led to the construction of large numbers of poorly conceived buildings. Nor is all of this frenzy strictly driven by the price of local oil and gas exports. Dubai, for example, was long a transit point for caravans on the trade route from Iraq to Oman, and for ships plying the waters between India, East Africa and the Northern Gulf. As the economic rise of the region came about, Dubai was well situated to become an international center of commerce where different cultures mixed. Its population consists mostly of expatriates, many of these from South Asia or South East Asia. Significantly, oil reserves in Dubai are less than one-twentieth of those of Abu Dhabi, for example, and oil income represents only a small part of the Emirate's income. The question of whether or not the remarkable upsurge of architectural activity in the Gulf should be considered positive or not might better be left to residents of the region and specialists in the ecological or financial consequences of such headlong development.

RAGS TO RICHES

The former Trucial States of the Gulf, located in the southeast of the Arabian Peninsula, granted England control of their defense and foreign affairs in 19th-century treaties. In 1971, six of these states—Abu Dhabi, 'Ajman, Dubai, Fujairah, Sharjah, and Umm al-Quwain—merged to form the United Arab Emirates (UAE). They were joined in 1972 by Ras al-Khaimah. Since the discovery of oil in the UAE more than thirty years ago, the country has undergone a profound transformation from an impoverished region of small desert emirates to a modern state with a high standard of living. With an economy expanding at over 10 percent a year and per capita GDP (up to $49 000 per person) as high as that of developed countries, the UAE have embarked on a remarkable program of urban and architectural expansion, in particular in Dubai and Abu Dhabi. The neighboring state of Qatar has been ruled by the al-Thani family since the mid-1800s. Under British domination like the UAE, it became an independent state in 1971. Doha, the state's capital, is also undergoing an extensive transformation, led by the construction of numerous office towers. The island kingdom of Bahrain, set in the Gulf to the northwest of Qatar, has a longer history of development and occupation. Oil was discovered there in 1932. With the British withdrawal in 1971, Bahrain, like its neighbors, became an independent state. Kuwait, at the northwestern corner of the Gulf, became the largest exporter of oil in the Gulf in 1953 and was the first of the Gulf States to declare its independence in 1961. Kuwait City's urban and architectural development was surely slowed by the events of the early 1990s, but it remains an example for the construction boom now occurring more to the south in the Gulf.

THE SHEIKH TAKES A LEAVE OF ABSENCE

An interesting case in the region is that of Qatar, holder of immense natural gas reserves (as well as an estimated 15 billion barrels of oil), and home to the headline-making regional television station Al-Jazeera. A vast and ambitious program of cultural development was undertaken there beginning in the late 1990s by a first cousin of Sheikh Hamad bin Khalifa al-Thani, the Emir of Qatar. Sheikh Saud al-Thani, as head of Qatar's National Council for Culture, Arts and Heritage, spent as much as $2.5 billion of public money on works of art to stock five museums and galleries he planned for Doha. Amongst these, only one, the Museum of Islamic Art by I. M. Pei, has actually gone forward, but the likes of Santiago Calatrava and Arata Isozaki were called in to design Western-style facilities in a city with few cultural attractions. Isozaki was to design a spectacular National Library, and he did lay out plans for an Education City, some of which has been built. Irregularities in the purchase of art works by Sheikh Saud led to his downfall and brief arrest, together with the halt of most of his projects. He apparently remains the client for

The rapidly changing skyline of Doha, the capital of the state of Qatar on the Gulf.

Die sich rasant verändernde Skyline von Doha, der Hauptstadt von Katar am Golf.

Le panorama urbain en transformation rapide de Doha, la capitale de l'état du Qatar au bord du Golfe Arabe.

the tower currently being built by Jean Nouvel in Doha, but his ambitious plans have largely been shelved. It remains that the Museum of Islamic Art will be the first world-class museum designed by a celebrated architect to open in the Gulf. It would appear, too, that Sheikh Saud's remarkable plans to put Doha on the map culturally speaking may well have influenced even more recent plans in the region.

THE ISLAND OF HAPPINESS

Despite the efforts of the Aga Khan over the years, it seems apparent that much, if not all, of what is being built in the Gulf has only limited connections to the rich traditions of Muslim architecture. Rather, the style chosen is that of the rapidly rising, the shiny, the new. Very often the architects involved in major developments would not be known to even the most assiduous followers of contemporary design. Large firms, developers who seem reticent to name architects even when they do have a good reputation, and above all large quantities of money seem to be the rule more often than not. However, although the pace of new projects and rising towers is such in the Emirates that it is difficult to generalize about architecture there, there are a number of encouraging signs that "quality" architecture is on the rise, first through the significant presence of major Western firms such as Skidmore, Owings & Merrill (SOM), HOK, Gensler or RNL (all present in this volume), and more recently with a number of "star" architects ranging from I. M. Pei to Frank Gehry, Zaha Hadid, Jean Nouvel, and Tadao Ando. In fact, the last four of these are all participating in what might be called the most ambitious architecture- and culture-driven project in the world. Saadiyat (Island of Happiness) off the coast of Abu Dhabi is a 27-square-kilometer development zone due for completion in 2018. With 150 000 residents, the island will be connected to the Abu Dhabi city via two causeways including a light-rail system. The 270-hectare Cultural District will include the Guggenheim Abu Dhabi, a modern and contemporary art museum being designed by Frank Gehry, the Classical Art Museum by Jean Nouvel which will operate in collaboration with the Louvre, a Performing Arts and Conference Center by Zaha Hadid, and the Maritime Museum by Tadao Ando. This ambitious set of buildings will be complemented by a series of 19 exhibition pavilions for the Abu Dhabi Biennale, designed by the likes of Greg Lynn, Asymptote and Pei-Zhu from China. The goal of this prestigious assemblage of talents, in a vast scheme slated to cost as much as $27 billion, is nothing less than to make Abu Dhabi into a cultural destination not only for the region but for the world. A reason for this concept is that it is currently estimated that the oil reserves of the Emirate will run out in 2046, leaving Abu Dhabi roughly 40 years to create a viable economy not based exclusively on the exploitation of fossil fuel reserves. It will come as no surprise that the man behind the line-up of star architects for this project is none other than Thomas Krens, Director of the Solomon R. Guggenheim Foundation and creator of the Guggenheim Bilbao, which has received no fewer than nine million visitors since it opened, created 4500 jobs for the local economy, and generated at least $2 billion in revenue for the city. Krens worked with SOM on the master plan for the district, while Gensler was responsible for a master plan for the entire island.

Nor is Saadiyat Island the only massive development district underway in Abu Dhabi. Reem Island, directly adjacent to the city of Abu Dhabi and just 200 meters from the shore, is the object of a master plan laid out by the architects RNL under the name Shams Abu Dhabi. RNL, also the master planners for the Burj Dubai area, aim at nothing less than the creation of a new city within the 156-hectare confines of their zone (one of three on Reem Island). The sheer size and ambition of these projects singles out Abu Dhabi, along with Dubai, as the center of the region's building boom. Indeed, well-known Western architects have been present in Abu Dhabi somewhat longer perhaps than in the other Emirates. Paul Andreu designed the airport there beginning in 1985, while Carlos Ott, designer of the Bastille Opera House in Paris, created the striking National Bank of Abu Dhabi headquarters between 1997 and 2000.

ONE FOR THE GUINESS

Carlos Ott was also the author of the National Bank of Dubai building (1996–98) with its characteristic wavelike form in reflective glass, but it might be that the current trend toward more and more spectacular buildings was led by the Burj Al Arab Hotel (1994–99) created by Tom Wright from the large English firm WS Atkins. Still the tallest hotel building in the world at 321 meters, its curved form sitting off the shores of Dubai may be the most frequently published image of Gulf architecture. A hotel reaching up over 300 meters for just 28 floors of double-height suites would seem to be no more than a stepping-stone toward the sort of projects that are today marking Dubai. Foremost amongst these is undoubtedly the Burj Dubai tower designed by Adrian Smith of SOM and destined to be the tallest freestanding structure in the world, surpassing the current record-holder, the 553-meter CN Tower in Toronto, and far above the Taipei 101 tower in Taiwan which measures "only" 509 meters. Very tall buildings have long exerted a fascination on the public and represented a significant symbol of economic power for the cities or countries that build them. Thus the Burj Dubai in some sense declares that the Dubai and the UAE are on the map as far as world affairs are concerned. Even if it appears that the myriad towers of Dubai are often built without very specific clients in mind, there is an overall pattern of attempting to use the vast financial liquidity generated not only in the Gulf but also in Russia or India, for example, to

Two views show the massive Saadiyat Island development project off the coast of Abu Dhabi, scheduled to be completed in 2012. Frank Gehry's Guggenheim is visible at the tip of the island, with the other museums jutting out into the water behind it.

Beide Perspektiven zeigen das riesige Entwicklungsgebiet der Insel Saadiyat vor der Küste Abu Dhabis. Die Planungen sollen bis 2012 umgesetzt werden. An der Inselspitze ist Frank Gehrys Guggenheim-Museum zu sehen, auf den Landzungen daneben weitere Museumsbauten.

Deux vues de l'énorme projet immobilier de l'île de Saadiyat face à Abu Dhabi, qui devrait être achevé en 2012. Le musée Guggenheim de Frank Gehry est visible à la pointe de l'île ; les autres musées se projettent sur l'eau, juste derrière.

create a new center for world trade. Perhaps encouraged not only by the rise in oil prices but also by a certain backlash against the United States after the fallout from the "war on terrorism," Dubai seeks to represent an alternative to New York or London for investors who have come from new horizons.

The Burj Dubai development is by no means the only one in this Emirate. Another large firm, Gensler, has laid out the plans for the Dubai International Financial Center (2001–04), a 1.85 million-square-meter 45-hectare complex of office buildings whose keynote building, The Gate, is a 90 000-square-meter arch built by the firm and intended to underline a "triumphal promenade reminiscent of the Champs-Elysées in Paris" inscribed in the Gensler master plan. The Gate symbolizes the "DIFC's permanence and stability," according to the architects and is amply symbolic of the yearning of the Gulf States to enter the select club of the financial and cultural centers of the world. Though some might say that this money would be better spent assisting poorer Muslim states, for example, the UAE has embarked on an effort to do nothing other than to create one or more cities on a par with Western capitals, minus their historic background.

BIG FOOTPRINT
All of this comes at a price of course. The World Wildlife Fund (WWF) published a report recently stating that the average resident of the Emirates puts a greater demand on the global ecosystem than even an average American. Then, too, the treatment of immigrant labor in Dubai and elsewhere in the Gulf has been the object of critical reports. As 3000 men work night and day to erect the tallest building in the world, fundamental questions can be raised of the role played by architecture in this far-reaching scheme to create a metropolis, or a world financial center, out of almost nothing. Adrian Smith, the designer of the Burj Dubai tower, admits that he was inspired by the towers of the Emerald City in the film version of *The Wizard of Oz.* "That was in my mind as I was designing Burj Dubai," he said, "although in a subliminal way." "I didn't research the way it looked. I just remembered the glassy, crystalline structure coming up in the middle of what seemed like nowhere. The funny thing is, I didn't remember it being green." The classic 1939 film based on L. Frank Baum's book *The Wonderful Wizard of Oz* of course chronicles the voyage of Dorothy, a young girl from Kansas played by Judy Garland in the movie, to the Emerald City, residence of the Wizard of Oz. Accompanied by a Lion, a Scarecrow and a Tin Woodsman, Dorothy first sees gleaming green towers at the edge of a forest: "There's Emerald City," she says. "Oh, we're almost there at last, at last! It's beautiful, isn't it? Just like I knew it would be. He really must be a wonderful Wizard to live in a city like that." But the great and powerful Wizard of

Oz turns out to be no more than a fraud, a "humbug," and the Emerald City the product of poppy-induced hallucinations. It might be noted that new areas such as DIFC are completely devoid of pedestrian areas; circulation is only in cars.

The remarkable development of Dubai, Abu Dhabi, Doha and other cities of the region is fueled by economic factors and the realization that fossil fuels are a finite resource that makes it incumbent on today's rulers to plan for tomorrow's inevitable post-oil economy. Architecture is playing a very important role in this transformation, be it in the symbolic reaching for the sky seen in the Burj Dubai, or in the cultural ambitions of Abu Dhabi for example. In the footsteps of architects like the airport builder Paul Andreu, or Carlos Ott in Dubai, the largest of Western firms, in the image of Gensler and HOK, follow. Whether or not all of this architecture can create the kind of "critical mass" necessary to generate real cities with the kind of financial and tourist activity that is only dreamed of today remains to be seen. In the meantime, the towers are rising.

Philip Jodidio

[1] L. Frank Baum, *The Wonderful Wizard of Oz*, George M. Hill Company, Chicago, 1900.

EINLEITUNG

DIE SMARAGDSTADT

»Den Reisegefährten wurde beinahe schwindlig von der Pracht, obgleich ihre Augen durch die Brillen geschützt waren. Die Häuser an den breiten Straßen waren aus grünem Marmor und mit funkelnden Smaragden besetzt. Das Pflaster bestand ebenfalls aus grünem Marmor und war in den Fugen mit dicht aneinandergesetzten Smaragden ausgelegt, die im hellen Licht des Tages glitzerten und schimmerten. Die Fensterscheiben der Häuser waren aus grünem Glas, der Himmel spannte sich hellgrün über die Stadt, und Dorothee kam es so vor, als leuchteten sogar die Sonnenstrahlen leicht grünlich.«

L. Frank Baum, *Der Zauberer von Oz*[1]

Nur wenige Gegenden auf der Welt können einen derart rasanten wirtschaftlichen Aufschwung wie die Emirate am Golf vorweisen. In einigen Städten am Golf – in jüngerer Zeit vor allem in Dubai, Abu Dhabi und Doha – hat sich ein beachtliches Baufieber ausgebreitet, und Hochhaustürme wachsen überall in den Himmel. Dabei sind ehrgeizige Bauprojekte in der Region nichts gänzlich Neues. Als das Oberhaupt der Ismailiten in den späten 1970er-Jahren den Aga-Khan-Preis für Architektur schuf, ging es ihm auch darum, ein Gegengewicht zu den seiner Meinung nach übereilt errichteten Gebäuden zu schaffen, die damals in Kuwait und anderswo entstanden und mit der Kultur des Landes nur wenig zu tun hatten. Selbst in den meisten westlichen Großstädten, etwa in New York, ist gute Architektur ja eher die Ausnahme als die Regel. Sicherlich hat die schwindelerregende Entwicklung der Golfemirate in den vergangenen Jahren zur Realisierung vieler unausgereifter Entwürfe geführt. Und nicht allein Öl- und Gaspreise tragen den Rausch. Dubai z. B. war lange Zeit eine Durchgangsstation für Karawanen, die auf den Handelswegen zwischen dem Irak und Oman unterwegs waren, sowie Anlaufstelle für die regelmäßig zwischen Indien, Ostafrika und dem Norden des Golfs verkehrenden Schiffe. Als der wirtschaftliche Aufschwung in der Region einsetzte, konnte Dubai von seiner günstigen Lage profitieren und wurde zu einem internationalen Handelszentrum, in dem sich die Kulturen mischten. Dubais Bevölkerung besteht im Wesentlichen aus Arbeitsmigranten aus Süd- und Südostasien. Bezeichnenderweise verfügt Dubai nur über weniger als ein Zwanzigstel der Ölvorräte von z. B. Abu Dhabi, und die Einkünfte aus dem Öl machen nur einen kleinen Teil der Einnahmen des Emirats aus. Die Beantwortung der Frage, ob der einzigartige Bauboom am Golf positiv oder negativ zu beurteilen ist, sollte man den Bewohnern oder den Spezialisten, die die ökologischen und finanziellen Konsequenzen der überhasteten Entwicklung beurteilen können, überlassen.

VOM TELLERWÄSCHER ZUM MILLIONÄR

Die ehemaligen Trucial States[2] am Golf im Südosten der Arabischen Halbinsel gewährten in den Verträgen des 19. Jahrhunderts den Engländern die Kontrolle über ihre Verteidigung und Außenpolitik. 1971 schlossen sich sechs dieser Staaten – Abu Dhabi, Ajman, Dubai, Fujaira, Sharja und Umm al-Kaiwain – zu den Vereinigten Arabischen Emiraten (VAE) zusammen. Ras al-Khaima folgte 1972. Seit der Entdeckung des Öls vor mehr als 30 Jahren hat ein tief greifender Wandel stattgefunden, der aus einer verarmten Region kleiner Wüstenemirate einen modernen Staat mit einem hohen Lebensstandard machte. Mit einem Wirtschaftswachstum von über 10 % im Jahr und einem Bruttoinlandsprodukt von bis zu 49 000 Dollar pro Kopf (dies entspricht dem BIP eines Industrielands) verfolgen die VAE seit einiger Zeit einen Kurs der Expansion ihrer Städte und der Realisierung immer größerer Bauprojekte. Dies gilt insbesondere für Dubai und Abu Dhabi. Der Nachbarstaat Katar wird seit Mitte des 19. Jahrhunderts von der Familie Al Thani regiert. Wie die ehemaligen Trucial States befand sich auch Katar zeitweilig unter britischer Herrschaft und wurde 1971 unabhängig. Doha, die Hauptstadt von Katar, erlebt derzeit einen starken Wandel durch den Bau einer Vielzahl von Bürohochhäusern. Der Inselstaat Bahrain nordwestlich von Katar entwickelte sich über einen längeren Zeitraum und war auch länger besetzt. 1932 wurde hier Öl entdeckt. Mit dem Abzug der Briten 1971 wurde Bahrain wie seine Nachbarstaaten unabhängig. Kuwait in der nordwestlichen Ecke des Golfs war 1953 größter Erdölexporteur am Golf und wurde 1961 als Erster der Golfstaaten unabhängig. Zwar hat sich seine städtebauliche und architektonische Entwicklung durch die Ereignisse Anfang der 1990er-Jahre verlangsamt, Kuwaits früherer Bauboom bleibt jedoch Vorbild für die Entwicklungen, die nun in den südlicheren Golfstaaten stattfinden.

EIN SCHEICH WIRD BEURLAUBT

Ein interessanter Fall in der Golfregion ist Katar. Neben schätzungsweise 15 Milliarden Barrel Öl verfügt es über riesige Gasreserven und ist Heimat des schlagzeilenträchtigen arabischen Fernsehsenders al-Djazira. Der Emir von Katar, ein direkter Cousin von Scheich Hamad Bin Khalifa al-Thani, verfolgt hier seit den späten 1990er-Jahren ein umfangreiches und ehrgeiziges kulturelles Entwicklungsprogramm. Scheich Saud Al Thani, Vorsitzender des Nationalen Rats für Kultur, Kunst und kulturelles Erbe, investierte nicht weniger als 2,5 Milliarden Dollar an öffentlichen Geldern in Kunstwerke, um mit ihnen fünf Museen und Ausstellungsräume, die er in Doha bauen wollte, auszustatten. Nur eines davon, das Museum für islamische Kunst von I. M. Pei, wurde tatsächlich gebaut. Auch Santiago Calatrava und Arata Isozaki planten in Doha, das sonst nur wenige kulturelle Attraktionen zu bieten hat, Einrichtungen westlicher Prägung. Isozaki entwarf die spektakuläre Nationalbi-

The Corniche in Abu Dhabi photographed in January, 2007 from the Breakwater Peninsula. To the right, the 165-meter-high Baynunah Hilton Tower.

Die Corniche in Abu Dhabi, fotografiert im Januar 2007 von der Breakwater-Halbinsel aus. Rechts im Bild der 165 m hohe Baynunah Hilton Tower.

La Corniche d'Abu Dhabi, photographiée en janvier 2007, depuis Breakwater. À droite, hôtel Hilton Baynunah, une tour de 165 m de haut.

bliothek und erstellte die städtebauliche Planung für die Education City, die bislang in Teilen realisiert wurde. Unregelmäßigkeiten beim Kauf der Kunstwerke brachten Scheich Saud zu Fall und führten zu seiner kurzzeitigen Inhaftierung und zum Stopp der meisten seiner Projekte. Offenbar ist er weiterhin der Bauherr des von Jean Nouvel entworfenen und derzeit im Bau befindlichen Hochhauses in Doha, der Rest seiner ehrgeizigen Pläne wurde jedoch größtenteils zu den Akten gelegt. Das Museum für islamische Kunst wird das erste Museum von Weltrang sein, das am Golf eröffnet wird und von einem Stararchitekten entworfen wurde. Auch scheint es so zu sein, dass Scheich Sauds aufsehenerregende Pläne, Doha in kultureller Hinsicht nach vorne zu bringen, Einfluss auf die jüngsten Planungen in der Region haben.

INSEL DES GLÜCKS

Trotz der langjährigen Bemühungen des Aga Khan bezieht sich vieles, wenn nicht alles, was am Golf gebaut wurde und wird, nur sehr bedingt auf die reiche Tradition muslimischer Architektur. Der gewählte »Stil« ist eher der des schnell in die Höhe Wachsenden, des Glänzenden, des Neuen. Sehr oft sind die Architekten, die hier große Entwicklungsgebiete planen, auch denen unbekannt, die alle aktuellen architektonischen Trends genau verfolgen. Große Büros, Projektentwickler, die die Architekten ihrer Projekte nicht nennen wollen, auch wenn diese einen guten Ruf genießen, und vor allem große Geldsummen sind die Regel. Die Geschwindigkeit, mit der in den Emiraten neue Projekte auftauchen und Türme in die Höhe wachsen, macht es schwierig, ein allgemeines Urteil über die Architektur abzugeben. Trotzdem gibt es eine Reihe optimistisch stimmender Zeichen, dass qualitätvolle Architektur im Kommen ist: Dazu gehören die starke Präsenz großer westlicher Firmen wie Skidmore, Owings & Merrill (SOM), HOK, Gensler oder RNL – alle sind in dieser Publikation vertreten – und, in jüngerer Zeit, die Beauftragung einer Reihe von Stararchitekten, darunter I. M. Pei, Frank Gehry, Zaha Hadid, Jean Nouvel und Tadao Ando. Die vier Letztgenannten sind die Architekten der wichtigsten Gebäude des ehrgeizigsten Architektur- und Kulturprojekts, das weltweit derzeit in Planung ist. Die Abu Dhabi vorgelagerte Insel Saadiyat (»Insel des Glücks«) ist ein 27 km² großes Entwicklungsgebiet, dessen Bebauung im Jahr 2018 abgeschlossen sein soll. Die Insel, auf der 150 000 Menschen leben sollen, wird über zwei Verbindungen, darunter eine Stadtbahn, mit Abu Dhabi verbunden sein.

Auf dem 270 ha großen Kulturareal sind derzeit folgende Bauten in Planung: das von Frank Gehry entworfene Guggenheim Abu Dhabi, ein Museum für moderne und zeitgenössische Kunst, das Museum für klassische Kunst von Jean Nouvel, das mit dem Louvre zusammenarbeiten wird, ein Theater- und Konferenzzentrum von Zaha Hadid sowie das Meeresmuseum von Tadao Ando. Ergänzt werden die-se ehrgeizigen Bauten durch 19 Pavillons, die als Ausstellungsorte der Abu Dhabi Biennale dienen sollen. Die Pavillons wurden u. a. von Greg Lynn, Asymptote und Pei-Zhu aus China entworfen. Das Ziel der Versammlung solch illustrer Talente ist nichts Geringeres, als Abu Dhabi nicht nur zu einem regionalen, sondern zu einem der weltweit führenden kulturellen Reiseziele zu machen. Die Kosten des gigantischen Vorhabens werden mit 27 Milliarden Dollar veranschlagt. Ein Motiv für diese Planungen sind aktuelle Schätzungen, wonach die Ölreserven der Emirate 2046 erschöpft sein werden. Abu Dhabi bleiben somit circa 40 Jahre, um eine tragfähige Wirtschaft aufzubauen, die nicht vollständig auf der Ausnutzung fossiler Brennstoffe basiert. Es überrascht nicht, dass Thomas Krens, Direktor der Solomon R. Guggenheim Foundation und Initiator des Guggenheim Bilbao, hinter der Beauftragung dieser Mannschaft von Stararchitekten steckt. Seit der Eröffnung haben 9 Millionen Besucher das Guggenheim Bilbao gesehen, 4500 Jobs wurden in der Region geschaffen, und Erträge von mindestens 2 Milliarden Dollar flossen der Stadt zu. SOM erstellte den Masterplan für den Kulturdistrikt, den Masterplan für die gesamte Insel erarbeitete das Büro Gensler.

Neben der Bebauung von Saadiyat sind in Abu Dhabi noch weitere Großprojekte im Entstehen. Direkt neben Abu-Dhabi-Stadt und nur 200 m von der Küste entfernt liegt die Insel Reem, für die RNL unter dem Namen Shams Abu Dhabi einen Masterplan erstellt haben. RNL, die auch den Masterplan für das Gebiet Burj Dubai erarbeitet haben, planen hier auf einem 156 ha großen Areal (eines von drei Baugebieten auf der Insel) gleich eine ganze neue Stadt. Die schiere Größe und die Ambitionen dieser Projekte machen Abu Dhabi neben Dubai zum Zentrum des Baubooms in der Golfregion, wobei renommierte westliche Architekten in Abu Dhabi vielleicht schon etwas länger tätig sind als in anderen Emiraten. Paul Andreu z. B. hat hier den Flughafen geplant, mit dessen Bau 1985 begonnen wurde; Carlos Ott, Architekt der Opéra Bastille in Paris, schuf zwischen 1997 und 2000 die beeindruckende Zentrale der Nationalbank von Abu Dhabi.

EIN TURM FÜR DAS GUINNESSBUCH

Auch der Entwurf für die Nationalbank von Dubai mit ihrer charakteristischen gewölbten Form aus reflektierendem Glas stammt von Carlos Ott (1996–98); den Trend zu immer spektakuläreren Gebäuden hat jedoch vermutlich das von Tom Wright vom großen englischen Planungsbüro WS Atkins entworfene Hotel Burj al-Arab (1994–99) in Gang gesetzt. Mit 321 m ist es immer noch das höchste Hotel der Welt. Wahrscheinlich wurde kein Gebäude am Golf häufiger publiziert als der vor der Küste von Dubai gelegene Hotelbau mit seiner bauchigen Silhouette. Allerdings war das über 300 m hohe Hotel mit nur 28 Geschossen mit

There are only occasional reminders that Dubai is in Arabia, such as the minarets seen in this image with the Emirates Towers visible to the left in the background. To the left, the foundation work for the Burj Dubai tower, March 2005.

Nur wenig erinnert daran, dass Dubai in Arabien liegt – etwa die Minarette hier im Bild. Im Hintergrund links die Emirates Towers. Linkes Bild: Fundamentarbeiten für den Burj Dubai im März 2005.

Seulement quelques rares éléments rappellent que Dubaï est en Arabie, comme les minarets que l'on voit sur cette image devant les Emirates Towers (à gauche au fond). À gauche, les travaux des fondations de la Burj Dubaï, en mars 2005.

doppelt hohen Suiten nur ein Meilenstein auf dem Weg zu den Projekten, die Dubai heute bestimmen. An erster Stelle steht dabei zweifellos der Burj Dubai, dessen Entwurf von Adrian Smith von SOM stammt. Er soll das höchste frei stehende Bauwerk der Welt werden und übertrifft den derzeitigen Rekordhalter, den 553 m hohen CN Tower in Toronto, und auch den Taipei 101 Tower in Taiwan, der »nur« 509 m hoch ist. Extrem hohe Gebäude faszinieren die Menschen schon lange. Sie sind ein bedeutendes Symbol der wirtschaftlichen Macht der Städte und Länder, in denen sie gebaut werden. Der Burj Dubai symbolisiert in gewisser Weise den Anspruch Dubais und der Vereinigten Arabischen Emirate auf eine globale Bedeutung. Auch wenn es scheint, als würden Dubais Myriaden von Hochhäusern oft ohne eine genaue Vorstellung der zukünftigen Nutzer gebaut werden, liegt dem der Versuch zugrunde, die gewaltige finanzielle Liquidität nicht nur der Golfregion, sondern z. B. auch Russlands und Indiens zu nutzen, um ein neues Zentrum des Welthandels zu schaffen. Unterstützt durch den gestiegenen Ölpreis und vielleicht auch durch antiamerikanische Reaktionen seit der Verkündung des »Kriegs gegen den Terrorismus« und dessen Begleiterscheinungen will Dubai für neu auftauchende Investoren eine Alternative zu New York und London bieten.

Der Burj Dubai ist keineswegs das einzige Großprojekt im Emirat Dubai. Ein anderes großes Büro, Gensler, hat das Dubai International Financial Center (DIFC, 2001–04) geplant, einen Bürokomplex mit 1,85 Millionen m² auf einem 45 ha großen Gelände, dessen Zentrum The Gate bildet, ein triumphbogenartiges Gebäude mit 46 000 m² Fläche. Es steht in der Achse einer »triumphalen Promenade, die an die Champs-Elysées in Paris« erinnert und ein wichtiges Element des Masterplans von Gensler ist. The Gate symbolisiert die »Beständigkeit und Stabilität des DIFC«, so die Architekten. In ihm manifestiert sich das Bestreben der Golfstaaten, zum auserwählten Kreis der Finanz- und Kulturzentren der Welt dazuzugehören. Man könnte einwenden, dass man z. B. das Geld besser dafür verwenden sollte, ärmere muslimische Länder zu unterstützen. Die Vereinigten Arabischen Emirate haben sich jedoch an keine geringere Aufgabe gemacht, als eine Stadt oder mehrere Städte zu schaffen, die – abgesehen von deren historischem Hintergrund – mit westlichen Hauptstädten gleichrangig sind.

GROSSE FUSSSTAPFEN

Dies alles hat natürlich seinen Preis. Der World Wildlife Fund (WWF) hat einen Bericht veröffentlicht, nach dem ein Bewohner der Emirate das globale Ökosystem im Durchschnitt noch stärker belastet als ein Nordamerikaner. Auch die Behandlung der Arbeitsmigranten in Dubai und anderen Golfregionen wurde kritisiert. 3000 Arbeiter arbeiten Tag und Nacht, um das weltweit größte Gebäude zu

errichten. In diesem Kontext ergeben sich grundsätzliche Fragen nach der Rolle, die die Architektur bei diesen weit in die Zukunft reichenden Vorhaben, eine Metropole oder ein Weltfinanzzentrum praktisch aus dem Nichts zu erschaffen, spielt.

Adrian Smith, Architekt des Burj Dubai, gesteht, dass die Türme der Smaragdstadt im Film »Der Zauberer von Oz« ihn zu seinem Entwurf inspirierten. Der Filmklassiker von 1939 nach dem Buch Der Zauberer von Oz von L. Frank Baum beschreibt bekanntlich die Reise von Dorothee, einem jungen Mädchen aus Kansas, zur Smaragdstadt, Wohnort des Zauberers von Oz. Sie sieht die funkelnden grünen Türme zum ersten Mal, als sie an einem Waldrand steht. »Da ist die Smaragdstadt!«, ruft sie. »Oh, wir sind fast da, endlich! Sie ist wunderschön, nicht wahr? Ich wusste, sie würde genau so aussehen. Er muss wirklich ein wunderbarer Zauberer sein, wenn er in solch einer Stadt lebt.« Später erweist es sich, dass der große und mächtige Zauberer von Oz nur Schwindel ist und die Smaragdstadt eine Folge von Halluzinationen, die durch Mohn hervorgerufen wurden. Anzumerken bleibt, dass es in den neuen Entwicklungsgebieten wie dem DIFC keine Fußgängerzonen gibt; die Erschließung erfolgt ausschließlich durch Autos.

Die beachtliche Entwicklung von Dubai, Abu Dhabi, Doha und anderen Städten in der Golfregion wird von wirtschaftlichen Faktoren und der Erkenntnis vorangetrieben, dass fossile Brennstoffe keine unendlich zur Verfügung stehenden Ressourcen sind. Letzteres macht es für die derzeitigen Herrscher zwingend erforderlich, für die Zeit nach dem Öl vorauszuplanen. Der Architektur kommt bei diesem Wandel eine überaus wichtige Rolle zu, sowohl was das Streben nach Höhe betrifft – wie etwa beim Burj Dubai – als auch im Hinblick auf die kulturellen Ambitionen, wie z. B. in Abu Dhabi. In die Fußstapfen des Flughafenarchitekten Paul Andreu oder in die von Carlos Ott in Dubai treten nun große westliche Büros, beispielsweise Gensler und HOK. Ob die neuen Gebäude die »kritische Masse« bilden können, die nötig ist, um echte Städte mit der finanziellen und touristischen Anziehungskraft zu schaffen, die man sich heute erträumt, wird sich erweisen. In der Zwischenzeit wachsen die Türme weiter in den Himmel.

Philip Jodidio

[1] L. Frank Baum, Der Zauberer von Oz, Cecilie Dressler Verlag, Hamburg, 1987
[2] In Deutschland als Piraten- oder Seeräuberküste bezeichnet.

INTRODUCTION

LA CITÉ D'ÉMERAUDE

« Bien que leurs yeux aient été protégés par des lunettes vertes, Dorothy et ses amis furent dans un premier temps éblouis par l'éclat de la merveilleuse Cité. Les rues étaient bordées de splendides maisons, toutes édifiées en marbre vert et piquetées d'émeraudes scintillantes. Ils marchaient sur un pavement du même marbre vert dont les dalles étaient jointées par des rangs d'émeraudes, finement serties, étincelantes sous l'éclat du soleil. Les carreaux des fenêtres étaient en verre vert, le ciel au-dessus de la ville était d'une nuance de vert, et même les rayons du soleil étaient verts. »

L. Frank Baum, *Le Magicien d'Oz*[1]

Peu de régions au monde peuvent se targuer d'un essor économique aussi rapide et important que celle des Émirats du Golfe. Une remarquable fièvre de construction s'est emparée de certaines villes – récemment Dubaï, Abu Dhabi et Doha – et des tours s'élèvent de tous les côtés. Cette volonté de projets ambitieux n'est cependant pas nouvelle dans cette région. Lorsqu'il créa le Prix d'architecture Aga Khan à la fin des années 1970, le chef de la communauté ismaélienne cherchait en partie à offrir des contre-propositions à cet engouement, qui consistait à construire des bâtiments dans l'urgence et dans les styles architecturaux sans racines culturelles qui sévissaient à l'époque au Koweït et ailleurs. On peut dire de la plupart des villes modernes, y compris de capitales occidentales comme New York, que l'architecture de qualité y est davantage l'exception que la règle, et il est certain que le vertigineux développement des Émirats du Golfe au cours de ces dernières années a poussé à l'édification d'un grand nombre d'immeubles pauvrement conçus. Cette frénésie n'est pas totalement liée au prix des exportations de pétrole et de gaz. Dubaï, par exemple, fut longtemps un centre de transit pour les caravanes sur la route entre l'Irak et l'Oman et pour les bateaux cabotant entre l'Inde, l'Afrique orientale et le nord du Golfe. Lorsque l'économie de la région prit les proportions que nous connaissons, la ville jouissait déjà d'une situation suffisamment favorable pour devenir un grand centre de commerce international où se croisaient différentes cultures. Sa population se compose essentiellement d'expatriés, dont beaucoup viennent du sud de l'Asie ou de l'Asie du Sud-Est. Il faut savoir que les réserves de pétrole de Dubaï représentent moins d'un vingtième de celle d'Abu Dhabi, par exemple, et que les ressources pétrolières ne constituent qu'une petite part de ses revenus. La question de savoir si l'étonnante efflorescence de l'activité architecturale dans le Golfe est un élément positif ou non doit être posée par les résidents de cette région et les spécialistes des impacts écologiques et financiers d'un développement aussi précipité.

DE LA PAUVRETÉ À LA RICHESSE

Les anciens États de la Trêve, au sud-est de la péninsule d'Arabie, avaient confié à la Grande-Bretagne leur défense et leur diplomatie dans des traités signés au XIXe siècle. En 1971, six de ces États – Abu Dhabi, Ajman, Dubaï, Fujaïrah, Charjah et Oumm al-Qaïwaïn) fusionnèrent pour constituer les Émirats arabes unis (EAU), rejoints en 1972 par le Ras el Khaïmah. Depuis la découverte de pétrole dans ces territoires il y a plus de trente ans, le pays a connu une transformation profonde, passant en quelques années du statut de petits émirats désertiques et pauvres à celui d'un état moderne bénéficiant d'un niveau de vie élevé. Avec un taux de croissance économique annuel de 10% et un revenu par habitant de plus de 49 000 dollars (USD), c'est-à-dire aussi élevé que celui des pays développés, les EAU ont lancé un remarquable programme d'expansion urbaine et de construction, en particulier à Dubaï et Abu Dhabi. L'État voisin du Qatar est dirigé par la dynastie des al-Thani depuis le milieu du XIXe siècle. Sous contrôle britannique, comme les EAU, il est devenu indépendant en 1971. Doha, sa capitale, connaît également une profonde transformation dont témoignent les chantiers de nombreuses tours de bureaux. L'histoire du développement de l'île Royaume de Bahreïn, dans le Golfe au nord-ouest du Qatar, est plus ancienne puisque du pétrole y a été découvert dès 1932. Après le retrait britannique en 1971, Bahreïn, comme ses voisins, est devenu indépendant. Le Koweït, au nord-ouest, est devenu le premier exportateur de pétrole du Golfe en 1953 et le premier état de la région à prendre son indépendance en 1961. Le développement urbanistique de Kuwait City a certainement été ralenti par les événements du début des années 1990, mais il reste exemplaire de cette croissance spectaculaire de la construction qui se poursuit aujourd'hui dans le sud de la région.

CHEIKH EN CONGÉ

Un cas particulièrement intéressant est celui du Qatar, détenteur d'immenses réserves de gaz naturel ainsi que de 15 milliards de barils de pétrole (estimation) et foyer de la célèbre télévision régionale Al-Jezira. À la fin des années 1990, un vaste et ambitieux programme de développement culturel a été lancé par un cousin germain du cheikh Hamad bin Khalifa al-Thani, l'émir du Qatar. Le cheikh Saoud al-Thani, président du Conseil national du Qatar pour la culture les arts et le patrimoine, a dépensé plus de 2,5 milliards de dollars de fonds publics en œuvres d'art pour remplir les cinq musées et galeries qu'il projetait d'édifier à Doha. Seul le projet de Musée d'art islamique de I. M. Pei a progressé, mais des architectes comme Santiago Calatrava et Arata Isozaki ont été eux aussi appelés pour concevoir des installations culturelles d'esprit occidental dans une ville qui en manquait singulièrement. Isozaki devait réaliser une spectaculaire bibliothèque nationale et

The Emirates Towers near Sheikh Zayed Road in Dubai. An area that was desert just a few years ago is today the center of a vibrant new city.

Die Emirates Towers in der Nähe der Sheikh Zayed Road in Dubai. Die Gegend, die noch vor ein paar Jahren Wüste war, ist heute Zentrum einer pulsierenden Stadt.

Les Emirates Towers près de la route Sheikh Zayed à Dubaï. Là où régnait encore le désert il y a à peine quelques années, se trouve le centre névralgique de la ville.

a proposé les plans d'une Cité de l'éducation dont quelques éléments ont été construits. Des irrégularités dans l'acquisition d'œuvres d'art par le cheikh Saoud al-Thani ont précipité sa chute, sa brève arrestation et le blocage de la plupart de ses projets. Il reste apparemment le commanditaire d'une tour qu'élève Jean Nouvel à Doha, mais ses ambitieux projets ont en grande partie été mis en sommeil. Il reste que le Musée d'art islamique sera le premier établissement de ce type et de classe internationale, conçu par un architecte célèbre, à ouvrir dans le Golfe. Il semble également que la dynamique créée par le cheikh pour faire parler de Doha dans le monde sur le plan culturel, a pu influencer d'autres projets régionaux.

L'ÎLE DU BONHEUR

Malgré les efforts déployés depuis de longues années par l'Aga Khan, on peut estimer qu'une grande partie, si ce n'est la totalité de ce qui se construit dans le Golfe n'entretient que de faibles liens avec les riches traditions architecturales musulmanes. Le style choisi tend plutôt vers le vite fait, la nouveauté, l'ostentatoire. Très souvent, les architectes appelés sont inconnus, y compris des amateurs informés de l'architecture contemporaine. C'est le règne des grosses agences, des promoteurs réticents à communiquer le nom des architectes, même s'ils ont une bonne réputation et de surcroît de l'argent en quantités énormes. Cependant, le rythme des nouveaux projets et des constructions de tours est tel qu'il est difficile de généraliser. Un certain nombre de signes encourageants montre que l'architecture « de qualité » est aujourd'hui un peu plus appréciée. C'est ce que semble indiquer l'arrivée de grandes agences occidentales, dont Skidmore, Owings & Merrill (SOM), HOK, Gensler ou RNL (toutes présentes dans ce volume) et, plus récemment, celle de quelques « stars », de I. M. Pei à Frank Gehry en passant par Zaha Hadid, Jean Nouvel et Tadao Ando. Plus concrètement, les quatre derniers cités participent à ce que l'on pourrait appeler le plus ambitieux projet culturel et architectural du monde : Saadiyat (l'Île du bonheur) sur la côte d'Abu Dhabi. Il s'agit d'une zone de 27 km² dont l'aménagement devrait être achevé en 2018. Peuplée de 150 000 habitants, cette île sera reliée à Abu Dhabi par deux levées, dont une réservée à un transport léger par rail. Le district culturel de 270 hectares comprendra le Guggenheim Abu Dhabi, un musée d'art moderne et contemporain conçu par Frank Gehry, le Musée d'art classique par Jean Nouvel, géré en collaboration avec le Louvre, un Centre de conférences et de spectacles par Zaha Hadid, et le Musée maritime de Tadao Ando. Cet ambitieux ensemble de bâtiments sera complété par une succession de dix-neuf pavillons d'expositions destinés à la Biennale d'Abu Dhabi, conçus par des architectes comme Greg Lynn, Asymptote ou le Chinois Pei-Zhu. L'objectif de cette prestigieuse réunion de talents et de cet investissement d'au moins 27 milliards de dollars n'est rien moins que de faire de

l'émirat une destination culturelle non seulement régionale mais mondiale. L'une des raisons de cette entreprise est que les réserves de pétrole locales devraient être épuisées en 2046, ce qui laisse environ quarante ans au pays pour mettre sur pied une économie viable ne reposant pas exclusivement sur l'exploitation des réserves fossiles. Il n'est pas surprenant que l'homme derrière cette parade d'architectes-stars soit le fameux Thomas Krens, directeur de la Fondation Solomon R. Guggenheim et créateur du Guggenheim Bilbao qui a reçu neuf millions de visiteurs depuis son ouverture, a suscité la création de 4500 emplois sur place et généré au moins 2 milliards de dollars de revenus pour la ville. Krens a travaillé avec SOM sur le plan directeur du district, Gensler étant le responsable de l'urbanisme de l'île tout entière.

L'île de Saadiyat n'est pas le seul projet massif en cours à Abu Dhabi. L'île de Reem, qui touche presque la capitale, à 200 m du rivage, est également l'objet d'un plan directeur des architectes de RNL, opération connue sous le nom de Chams Abu Dhabi. RNL, également chargée de l'urbanisme de la zone de la Burj Dubai, propose la création d'une nouvelle ville sur 156 hectares alloués (une des trois zones répartie sur l'île de Reem). Les dimensions impressionnantes et l'ambition de ces projets font d'Abu Dhabi, ainsi que de Dubaï, le centre du boom de la construction dans le Golfe. Des architectes occidentaux connus sont présents sur place depuis plus longtemps que dans les autres émirats. Paul Andreu y a construit l'aéroport dès 1985, et Carlos Ott, auteur de l'Opéra Bastille à Paris, a conçu l'étonnant siège de la Banque nationale d'Abu Dhabi (1997–2000).

UN AUTRE RECORD POUR LE GUINNESS

Carlos Ott est également le signataire de l'immeuble de la Banque nationale de Dubaï (1996-98) en forme de vague très particulière et en verre réfléchissant, mais il se peut que la tendance actuelle vers des bâtiments de plus en plus spectaculaires ait été lancée par l'hôtel Burj Al Arab (1994–99), œuvre de Tom Wright, architecte de la grande agence britannique WS Atkins. Encore aujourd'hui, cet hôtel de 321 m, le plus haut du monde, avec sa forme incurvée qui se dresse en bordure de la côte, est sans doute l'image de l'architecture du Golfe la plus publiée. Un hôtel de plus de 300 mètres pour seulement vingt-huit niveaux de suites en duplex pourrait sembler maintenant presque banal par rapport aux projets auxquels Dubaï réfléchit aujourd'hui. Le plus important d'entre eux certainement la Burj Dubaï (Tour de Dubaï) conçue par Adrian Smith (SOM), sera la plus haute construction du monde et dépassera les 553 mètres de la CN Tower de Toronto et la tour 101 de Taipei qui ne mesure « que » 509 mètres. Les immeubles de très grande hauteur exercent depuis toujours une fascination sur le public et symbolisent visuellement la

The Burj Dubaï Tower in Dubai became the tallest
man-made structure in the world in September 2007
during its construction.

Im September 2007, noch während der Burj Dubai in Dubai
im Bau war, wurde er zum höchsten Bauwerk der Welt.

Encore en construction (ici en septembre 2007),
le Burj Dubaï deviendra le plus haut gratte-ciel au monde.

puissance économique des villes ou des pays qui les édifient. Ainsi le Burj Dubaï proclame que les Émirats arabes unis sont des partenaires avec qui compter, du moins sur le plan des affaires. Même s'il semble que la myriade de tours de Dubaï soient souvent construites sans penser à un quelconque client spécifique, on comprend la volonté d'utiliser les énormes liquidités financières générées non seulement dans le Golfe, mais aussi en Russie ou en Inde, par exemple, pour créer un nouveau grand centre du commerce international. Encouragé par l'augmentation des prix du pétrole et aussi peut-être par une certaine réaction contre les États-Unis après les déconvenues de la « guerre au terrorisme », Dubaï cherche à offrir une alternative à New York ou Londres à des investisseurs venus de nouveaux horizons.

La Burj Dubaï n'est pas le seul grand projet de développement en cours dans cet émirat. Une autre grande agence, Gensler, a conçu les plans du Centre financier international de Dubaï (2001–04), complexe de 1,85 million de m² de bureaux sur 45 hectares comprenant « The Gate » (la porte), arc de 90 000 m² édifié par l'agence, et qui signale « une promenade triomphale rappelant les Champs-Élysées à Paris » prévue dans le plan directeur d'urbanisme de Gensler. Cette porte symbolise la « permanence et la stabilité du DIFC (Dubaï International Financial Center) », selon les architectes, et l'ambition des états du Golfe d'entrer dans le très sélect club des centres financiers et culturels de la planète. Bien que certains pensent que cet argent serait mieux investi dans l'aide aux pays musulmans pauvres, par exemple, les EAU ont fait le choix de lancer ce programme qui consiste très concrètement à créer une ou plusieurs villes qui puissent rivaliser avec les capitales occidentales, moins leur passé historique bien sûr.

L'EMPREINTE GÉANTE

Tout ceci a son prix. Le World Wildlife Fund (WWF) a récemment publié un rapport qui établit que le résident moyen des Émirats exerce sur l'écosystème global une pression plus forte que celle de l'Américain moyen lui-même. Le traitement de la main-d'œuvre immigrée à Dubaï et dans d'autres pays du Golfe a également fait l'objet de rapports critiques. Lorsque 3000 hommes travaillent jour et nuit pour ériger l'immeuble le plus haut du monde, des questions fondamentales peuvent être posées sur le rôle joué par l'architecture dans ces projets extrêmes qui veulent créer une métropole ou un centre financier international à partir de pratiquement rien. Adrian Smith, concepteur de la Burj Dubaï, admet qu'il a été inspiré par les tours de la Cité d'émeraude de la version filmée du *Magicien d'Oz* : « Je l'avais en tête lorsque je dessinais la Burj Dubaï, bien que de façon subliminale... Je ne suis pas allé voir à quoi tout cela ressemblait. Je me souvenais seulement de constructions cristallines s'élevant au milieu de ce qui n'avait l'air de rien. La chose

amusante est que je ne me souvenais pas de la couleur verte. » Le film classique de 1939, d'après le livre éponyme de L. Frank Baum, rapporte les pérégrinations de Dorothy, une petite fille du Kansas interprétée par Judy Garland dans le film, vers la Cité d'émeraude, résidence du magicien. Accompagnée d'un lion, d'un épouvantail et d'un homme en fer blanc, elle aperçoit pour la première fois ces tours vertes étincelantes à la lisière de la forêt : « Voici la Cité d'émeraude, dit-elle, nous sommes presque arrivés, enfin, enfin ! C'est splendide, n'est-ce pas ? Exactement comme je savais que ce serait. Ce doit être vraiment un merveilleux magicien pour vivre dans une cité comme celle-ci ! » Mais le grand et puissant magicien d'Oz se révèle être un charlatan, et la Cité d'émeraude le produit d'hallucinations provoquées par des pavots. Il faut noter que les nouveaux quartiers évoqués plus haut, comme celui du DIFC, ne laissent aucune place aux piétons. La circulation ne pouvant se faire qu'en voiture.

Le remarquable développement de Dubaï, Abu Dhabi, Doha et d'autres villes de la région est alimenté par des facteurs économiques et la prise de conscience que les ressources fossiles ne sont qu'une ressource limitée qui impose à leurs souverains actuels de prévoir l'économie d'après le pétrole. L'architecture joue un rôle très important dans cette transformation, que ce soit symboliquement dans le cas de la course aux sommets dont la construction de la Burj Dubaï témoigne, ou culturellement dans les ambitions d'Abu Dhabi, par exemple. Sur les pas d'architectes tels que le constructeur d'aéroport Paul Andreu ou Carlos Ott à Dubaï, les plus grandes agences occidentales, comme Gensler ou HOK, ont suivi. Il reste à voir si cette architecture pourra créer cette « masse critique » à partir de laquelle on peut parler de vraie ville vivant de l'activité financière et touristique dont on rêve encore aujourd'hui. Pendant ce temps, des tours s'élèvent...

Philip Jodidio

[1] L. Frank Baum. *Le Magicien d'Oz*, Folio Junior, Paris, 1998.

AEDAS

AEDAS LTD.
19/F, 1063 King's Road, Quarry Bay
Hong Kong
China

Tel: +852 2861 1728
Fax: +852 2529 6419
e-mail: hongkong@aedas.com
Web: www.aedas.com

Currently the fourth-largest architectural practice in the world, **AEDAS** has over 1700 staff members in 26 offices in London, Hong Kong, and New York, as well as in China, Singapore, India, Kazakhstan, the United Arab Emirates, Russia, Poland, and Brazil. The firm provides expertise in architecture, interior design, urban design, landscape, building survey and graphic design across a diverse range of project types. The firm is carrying out numerous projects in the UAE, particularly in Dubai and Abu Dhabi. Andrew Bromberg, the Executive Director of Aedas in Hong Kong, joined the company in 2002. His current projects in the UAE include DAMAC Ocean Heights I at Dubai Marina, an 82-story residential development (2005–08); Dancing Towers, an 81 000-square-meter mixed-use development comprising retail, office, serviced apartment and hotel, Dubai (2005–08); Boulevard Plaza, Dubai, two towers at the gateway into the Burj Dubai development (2005–09); DAMAC Ocean Heights II at Dubai Marina, a competition-winning design for a 106-story residential development (2006–10); U-BORA Tower Business Bay, Dubai (2006–10); the Empire Tower in Shams, Abu Dhabi, a residential development (2006–); and the Oceanscape at Shams, Abu Dhabi, a large-scale residential and mixed-use development with a total site area of approximately 134.6 hectares (2006–); as well as the projects published here.

DANCING TOWERS
ABU DHABI, UAE
2005-10

AREA: 51 748 m²
SITE AREA: 4180 m²
CLIENT: Capital Investment
COST: not disclosed

The difficulty presented by this project had to do with its large size as compared to relatively small neighboring buildings in the heart of Abu Dhabi. Essentially designed for furnished apartments (18 315 m²) and an office tower (28 826 m²), the structure will also contain a small amount of retail and recreational space (4 607 m²), basically divided into commercial and residential towers connected by a retail podium. Although the division into two towers was a partial response to the question of the relationship to the existing neighborhood, the tight site suggested the undulating forms of the buildings. The architects explain, "The two towers quickly lean, rotate, bend and warp to respond to each other, the adjacent sites, and ultimately the view to the ocean at their horizon. These two figures fluidly respond to each other, dynamically engaged and flowing—ultimately tied together in a passionate dance." Although unexpected forms have become the norm in the United Arab Emirates in the course of their recent rapid urban development, these buildings retain the same elegance shown by Andrew Bromberg and Aedas for the Pentominium also published here.

Die Schwierigkeit dieses Projektes lag in seiner Größe – die Nachbargebäude im Zentrum Dubais sind vergleichsweise klein. Der Bau soll im Wesentlichen möblierte Apartments (18 315 m²), einen Büroturm (28 826 m²) sowie einen kleinen Anteil an Laden- und Freizeitflächen (4607 m²) enthalten. Dieses Programm wird in einen Wohnturm und einen Turm mit kommerzieller Nutzung aufgeteilt; ein Sockel mit Ladenflächen verbindet die beiden Bauten. Die Aufteilung in zwei Baukörper war auch eine Reaktion auf die Frage der Beziehung zu den benachbarten Gebäuden. Die wellenförmige Form dagegen resultiert aus dem engen Grundstück. Die Architekten erläutern: »Die beiden Türme neigen und drehen sich, sie beugen und biegen sich und reagieren aufeinander, auf die Nachbargebäude und letztlich auch auf das Meer. Die Figuren beziehen sich geschmeidig, dynamisch und fließend aufeinander – zusammen tanzen sie einen leidenschaftlichen Tanz.« Durch die rasante Entwicklung der Städte in den Vereinigten Arabischen Emiraten sind außergewöhnliche Formen dort mittlerweile Standard. Darüber hinausgehend wohnt den Dancing Towers wie dem ebenfalls von Andrew Bromberg/Aedas entworfenen Pentominium eine besondere Eleganz inne.

La difficulté de ce projet tenait à ses grandes dimensions par rapport aux immeubles voisins de relativement faible hauteur du centre d'Abu Dhabi. Essentiellement conçu pour accueillir des appartements meublés (18 315 m²) et un tour d'affaires (28 826 m²), l'immeuble contiendra également une petite nombre de commerces et de l'espace de recréation (4607 m²) répartis entre une tour résidentielle et une tour de bureaux, réunies par un podium réservé aux magasins. Bien que la division en deux tours soit une réponse partielle aux relations avec le voisinage, c'est l'étroitesse du site qui a inspiré la forme onduleuse des deux structures. Selon les architectes : « Les deux tours s'inclinent, pivotent, se tordent et se drapent pour dialoguer entre elles, mais aussi avec les sites adjacents et la vue sur l'océan à l'horizon. Ces deux figures se répondent l'une à l'autre de manière fluide, dans un dialogue dynamique qui fusionne au final dans une danse passionnée. » Bien que les formes surprenantes soient quasi la norme dans les Émirats arabes unis durant cette période de développement urbain accéléré, ces immeubles conservent la même élégance que le Pentominium d'Andrew Bromberg et Aedas, également publié dans ces pages.

PENTOMINIUM
DUBAI, UAE
2006-11

AREA: 116 200 m²
CLIENT: Trident International Holdings
COST: not disclosed

The Pentominium building, located in Dubai Marina, could be the tallest residential tower in the world at 516 meters. Given that the city is reaching to even greater heights in towers such as the Burj Dubai, it has become increasingly difficult for architects to make the kind of marked presence felt on the skyline that many clients demand. In this instance, the light, elegant silhouette of the structure will surely be identifiable no matter what the urban environment. The design seeks to respond to specific site conditions, "the density/proximity of the neighbors, and the extreme environment pressures of Dubai." The slender building has two different sides that share a central core: one, southern-oriented, has a gently spiraling vertical layer of glass and balconies to "mitigate solar gain," while the other displays a staggered form, "alternating between apartments and voids of sky-gardens." Six five-story pods are attached to the core and project from its surface allowing the tower to "breathe," according to the architect. An observation deck is planned at an altitude of 400 meters and a swimming pool on the next level down, 396 meters above the ground.

Das Pentominium in der Dubai Marina mit einer geplanten Höhe von 516 m könnte das höchste Wohnhochhaus der Welt werden. Weil die Stadt mit Türmen wie dem Burj Dubai immer weiter in die Höhe strebt, wird es für die Architekten zunehmend schwieriger, ihren Gebäuden die von vielen Bauherren geforderte Präsenz in der Skyline von Dubai zu verschaffen. Wie auch immer sich seine Umgebung entwickeln wird – die lichte, elegante Silhouette des Pentominium wird ganz bestimmt auffallen. Der Entwurf versucht auf die speziellen Gegebenheiten des Standorts, »die Dichte/Nähe der Nachbargebäude und die extremen klimatischen Bedingungen Dubais« zu reagieren. Das schlanke Gebäude besteht aus zwei verschiedenen Hälften, die sich an einen gemeinsamen Kern anlagern. Die Südseite ist mit einer über die Höhe des Turms leicht verdrehten Schicht aus Glas und Balkonen versehen, »die die Aufheizung durch die Sonne reduzieren soll«, die Nordseite dagegen hat ein kammförmiges Profil, »bei dem sich Appartements und Himmelsgärten abwechseln«. Sechs jeweils fünfgeschossige Volumen kragen vom Gebäudekern aus und lassen den Turm »atmen«, wie die Architekten erläutern. In 400 m Höhe ist eine Aussichtsplattform, im Geschoss darunter – 396 m über dem Erdboden – ein Swimmingpool geplant.

Le Pentominium à Dubaï Marina qui culmine à 516 m est sans doute la plus haute tour résidentielle du monde. La réglementation locale acceptant des « altitudes » encore supérieures, comme pour la Burj Dubaï par exemple, il est de plus en plus difficile pour des architectes d'imaginer des projets dont la présence puisse marquer le panorama urbain, attente de nombreux clients. Ici, cette silhouette légère et élégante restera certainement identifiable quoique devienne son futur environnement. La conception a cherché à répondre aux conditions spécifiques du site, à « la densité et à la proximité des immeubles voisins et aux pressions environnementales extrêmes que connaît Dubaï ». Cet immeuble élancé présente deux faces différentes autour d'un noyau commun. La façade ouest est animée d'un mouvement en spirale de strates de parois vitrées et de balcons destinés à « réduire le gain solaire », tandis que l'autre prend une forme étagée « alternant les apartements et les vides des jardins suspendus ». Six *pods* de cinq niveaux sont rattachés à ce noyau et se projettent au-dessus du vide, ce qui permet à la tour de « respirer », selon l'architecte. Une plate-forme d'observation devrait être aménagée à 400 m d'altitude et une piscine à 396 m.

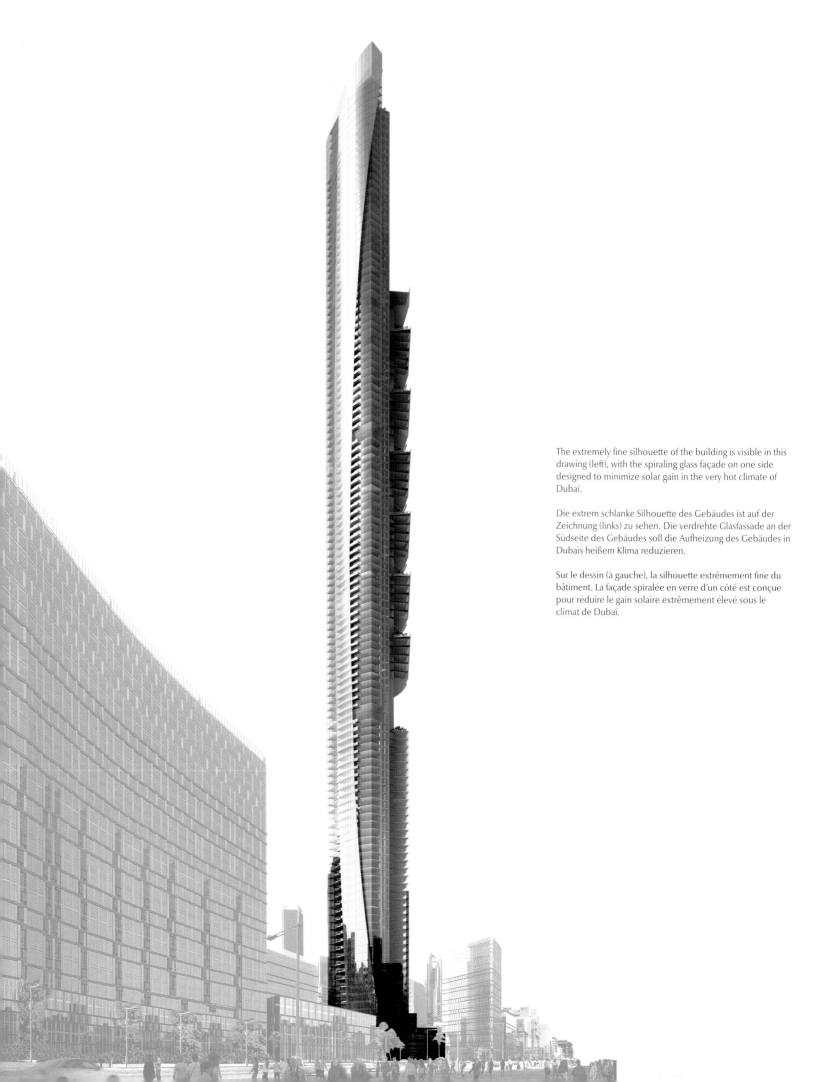

The extremely fine silhouette of the building is visible in this drawing (left), with the spiraling glass façade on one side designed to minimize solar gain in the very hot climate of Dubai.

Die extrem schlanke Silhouette des Gebäudes ist auf der Zeichnung (links) zu sehen. Die verdrehte Glasfassade an der Südseite des Gebäudes soll die Aufheizung des Gebäudes in Dubais heißem Klima reduzieren.

Sur le dessin (à gauche), la silhouette extrêmement fine du bâtiment. La façade spiralée en verre d'un côté est conçue pour réduire le gain solaire extrêmement élevé sous le climat de Dubaï.

A floor plan and section of the building show the suspended pods on one side of the building as well as the facilities planned on the upper levels such as an observation deck and swimming pool located almost 400 meters above the ground.

Grundriss und Schnitt zeigen die auskragenden Volumen auf der einen Seite des Turms sowie die in den oberen Geschossen geplanten Angebote, z. B. eine Aussichtsplattform und einen Swimmingpool fast 400 m über dem Erdboden.

Un plan de niveau et une coupe de la tour montrent les *pods* suspendus latéralement et les équipements prévus aux niveaux supérieurs, dont une terrasse d'observation et une piscine à près de 400 m au-dessus du niveau du sol.

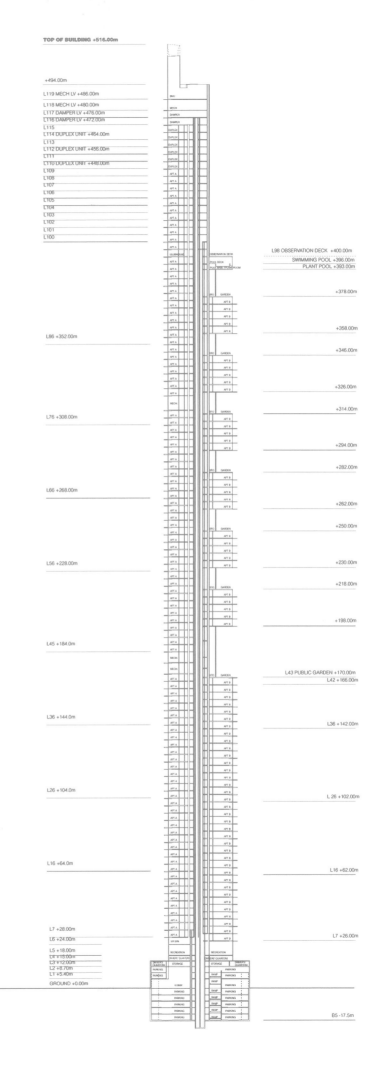

2

TADAO ANDO

**TADAO ANDO ARCHITECT
& ASSOCIATES**

Osaka 531-0072
Japan

Born in Osaka in 1941, **TADAO ANDO** was self-educated as an architect, largely through his travels in the United States, Europe and Africa (1962–69). He founded Tadao Ando Architect & Associates in Osaka in 1969. He has received the Alvar Aalto Medal, Finnish Association of Architects (1985); Medaille d'or, French Academy of Architecture (1989); the 1992 Carlsberg Prize; and the 1995 Pritzker Prize. He has taught at Yale (1987), Columbia (1988) and at Harvard (1990). Notable buildings include: Rokko Housing, Kobe, Japan (1983–93); Church on the Water, Hokkaido, Japan (1988); Japan Pavilion Expo '92, Seville, Spain (1992); Forest of Tombs Museum, Kumamoto (1992); and the Suntory Museum, Osaka (1994), both in Japan. Recent work includes the Awaji Yumebutai, Awajishima, Hyogo, Japan (1997–2000); the Pulitzer Foundation for the Arts, St. Louis, Missouri (1997–2000); and the Modern Art Museum of Fort Worth, Fort Worth, Texas, United States (1999–2002). He completed the Chichu Art Museum on the Island of Naoshima in the Inland Sea in 2003, part of the continuing project that led him to create the Benesse House museum and hotel there beginning in the early 1990s. He won the competition to design the Pinault Foundation on the Ile Seguin, in Paris, France, but the project was cancelled in 2005, and he subsequently remodeled Palazzo Grassi in Venice, Italy, for the French arts patron. More recent work includes the hhstyle.com building, Tokyo (2004–05); and the nearby Omote-Sando Hills project (1996–2006). He is currently working on Rokko IV, Kobe (2004–); 21-21 Design Sight (with Issey Miyake, 2003–07); and the Tokyu Shibuya Station, Tokyo (2005–08), all in Japan.

MARITIME MUSEUM
ABU DHABI, UAE
2006 -

FLOOR AREA: 33 300 m²
CLIENT: Tourism Development and Investment
Company of Abu Dhabi (TDIC),
Solomon R. Guggenheim Foundation
COST: not disclosed

Part of the ambitious new projects planned on Saadiyat Island off the coast of Abu Dhabi, Tadao Ando's Maritime Museum will have an exposed concrete finish. Its main building will be 108 meters long, 36 meters wide and 27 meters high, dominating its 61 000-square-meter site jutting out into the waters of the Arabian Gulf. The structure arches dramatically over a water court intended to symbolize the meeting of Abu Dhabi's water and land. The basic volume is meant to give the impression that it has been carved from a solid mass by the wind, while the surrounding landscape is organized in a grid pattern. Rows of trees mark the transition from the future city on Saadiyat Island and the calmer, more contemplative architecture of Ando. The maritime theme of the structure is developed inside, as the architect explains:, "Within the ship-like interior of the volume, ramps and floating decks guide visitors fluidly through the exhibition space, echoing the theme of the museum and creating a dynamic gallery experience. Dhows float over the voids of the interior space and help create an intense visual experience by relating objects to one another and to the museum architecture as a whole. Below ground, there is a second space—a reception hall with an enormous aquarium. A traditional dhow floats over the aquarium and is seen from different perspectives."

Tadao Andos Meeresmuseum ist eines der ehrgeizigen Projekte, die auf der Abu Dhabi vorgelagerten Insel Saadiyat realisiert werden sollen. Alle Außenflächen bestehen aus Sichtbeton. Das Hauptgebäude wird eine Länge von 108 m, eine Breite von 36 m und eine Höhe von 27 m haben. Es wird das 61 000 m² große Grundstück dominieren und in den Golf hineinragen. Der Baukörper schwingt sich dramatisch über einen »Wasserhof«, der das Aufeinandertreffen der Elemente Wasser und Land in Abu Dhabi symbolisieren soll. Es soll der Eindruck entstehen, der Wind hätte die Form des Baukörpers aus einem massiven Block ausgehöhlt. Das Gelände in der Umgebung des Museums ist rasterartig gegliedert; Baumreihen markieren den Übergang zwischen der zukünftigen Stadt auf Saadiyat und der ruhigeren, kontemplativen Architektur Andos. Wie der Architekt erläutert, wird das ma-

ritime Thema im Inneren des Gebäudes entwickelt: »Im schiffsähnlichen Innenraum leiten Rampen und schwebende Decks die Besucher fließend durch den Ausstellungsraum, lassen das Thema des Museums widerhallen und schaffen ein dynamisches Ausstellungserlebnis. Dauen schweben in der Luft und unterstützen das intensive visuelle Erlebnis, indem sie Ausstellungsobjekte miteinander und zur Museumsarchitektur in Beziehung setzen. Im Untergeschoss gibt es einen weiteren Raum, ein Eingangsfoyer mit einem riesigen Aquarium. Über dem Aquarium schwebt eine traditionelle Dau, die aus verschiedenen Perspektiven betrachtet werden kann.«

Composant important des ambitieux projets prévus dans l'île de Saadiyat sur la côte d'Abu Dhabi, le Musée maritime de Tadao Ando a opté pour le béton brut. Le bâtiment principal de 108 m de long, 36 m de large et 27 m de haut s'élèvera sur un terrain de 61 000 m² en avancée sur le Golfe Arabe. L'arc spectaculaire formé au-dessus de la cour-bassin symbolise la rencontre de la mer et de la terre à Abu Dhabi. Le volume semble avoir été sculpté par le vent dans un bloc massif. Son environnement sera organisé selon une grille. Des alignements d'arbres feront transition entre la future ville de l'île de Saadiyat et l'architecture plus calme et plus contemplative de l'architecte japonais. Ando explique que le thème maritime se retrouve aussi à l'intérieur : « Comme dans un bateau, des rampes et des terrasses suspendues orientent le flux des visiteurs à travers les espaces d'expositions, en écho à la thématique muséale pour créer une expérience dynamique de la contemplation des pièces présentées. Des « dhow » (bateaux traditionnels) sont supendus au-dessus des grands vides du volume interne et contribuent à cette expérience visuelle intense qui relie les objets les uns aux autres et à l'architecture globale du musée. En sous-sol, se trouve un second volume, le hall de réception doté d'un énorme aquarium. Un « dhaun flotte sur l'aquarium et peut être vu sous différentes perspectives. »

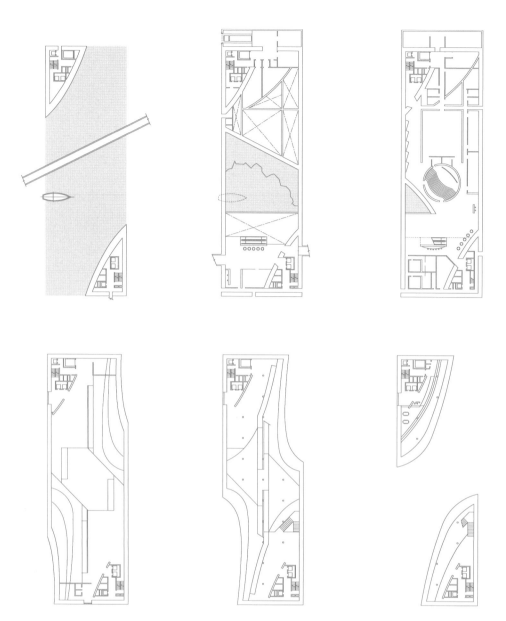

The unexpected, flowing design of Ando's museum will allow it both to symbolically incarnate the maritime image implied in its function and to offer spectacular views of the Gulf.

Andos überraschende, fließende Formen thematisieren einerseits Bilder, die der Funktion des Gebäudes als Meeresmuseum entsprechen, andererseits bietet der Entwurf spektakuläre Ausblicke auf den Golf.

Les contours fluides du musée d'Ando symbolisent le contenu de ce musée maritime et permettent de dégager des vues spectaculaires sur le Golfe.

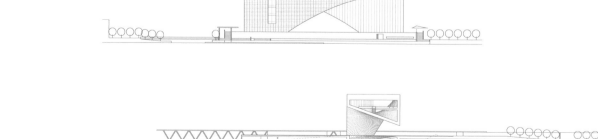

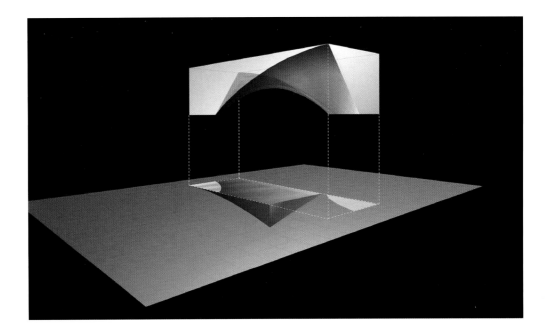

With its carved central void, the museum is open to its environment, but devices such as viewing platforms will emphasize the surrounding water as well.

Der wie herausgeschnitten wirkende zentrale Außenraum des Museums öffnet sich zum Wasser, aber auch andere Elemente, etwa die Aussichtsplattformen, betonen den Bezug zum Meer.

Le musée s'ouvre sur son environnement par un énorme vide central sculpté. Des équipements comme des plates-formes d'observation mettront également en valeur la présence de l'eau.

3

ASYMPTOTE

ASYMPTOTE ARCHITECTURE GROUP
160 Varick Street, Floor 10
New York, NY 10013
United States

Tel: +1 212 343 7333
Fax: +1 212 343 7099
e-mail: info@asymptote.net
Web: www.asymptote.net

HANI RASHID received his M.Arch degree from the Cranbrook Academy of Art, Bloomfield Hills, Michigan. He is presently a Professor of Architecture at Columbia University in New York and at the Swiss Federal Institute of Technology (ETH) in Zurich. He is also a member of the Steering Committee of the Aga Khan Award for Architecture. Lise Anne Couture was born in Montreal in 1959. She received her B.Arch degree from Carlton University, Canada, and her M.Arch degree from Yale. Couture currently holds the Davenport chair at Yale University School of Architecture. They created Asymptote in 1987. Projects include their 1988 prize-winning commission for the Los Angeles West Coast Gateway (1989); a commissioned housing project for Brig, Switzerland; and their participation in the 1993 competition for an Art Center in Tours, France (1993). More recent work by Asymptote includes a theater festival structure built in Denmark in 1997; a virtual trading floor for the New York Stock Exchange; and the Guggenheim Virtual Museum, a multimedia project aimed at creating an online museum. In 2001, Asymptote participated in competitions for the Daimler-Chrysler and Mercedes-Benz Museums in Stuttgart, Germany, an expansion of the Queen's Museum, and the Eyebeam Center in New York. Most recently Asymptote completed the construction of Hydra-Pier in Harlemmermeer, The Netherlands, a public building housing technology and art located near Schipol Airport. They also finished the Carlos Miele Flagship Store on West 14th Street in Manhattan in 2003. Asymptote was involved in the design of the 2004 Venice Biennale of Architecture, "Metamorph," and a new theater for the Hans Christian Andersen festival in Odense, Denmark. Asymptote designed the Beukenhof Crematorium and Memorial Chapel in Rotterdam, The Netherlands; recently completed the Alessi Flagship Store in the SoHo area of Manhattan; and are currently working on the Mutiara Complex in Penang, Malaysia.

STRATA TOWER
ABU DHABI, UAE
2005 - 09

FLOOR AREA: 51 500 m²
CLIENT: not disclosed
COST: not disclosed

This 50-story tower is due to be the tallest building in the Al Raha Beach development. Hani Rashid explains, "The tower's architecture is neither symbolic nor narrative, but rather seeks meaning through an abstract use of form and dynamic movement to work with the environment, the light, sea, and atmospheres that envelop this magical place on the Arabian Sea. The flow and movement of the surface affords the architecture its iconic status without being an overt gesture or building reliant on a set meaning or association. Rather, the mathematical procedures used, not unlike those in the manifestation of the arabesque or abstract Islamic calligraphy, afford the building its elegance and musicality." Meant for luxurious residences, the building's design is also based on the flowing computer-designed style of the New York architects. Despite the large number of buildings being erected in the UAE, few are as evocative of architectural quality as this one, a sign of the times surely because Abu Dhabi seems to have seen the interest of increasing the design excellence of its new structures.

Der 50-geschossige Turm soll das höchste Gebäude des Entwicklungsgebiets Al-Raha Beach werden. »Die Architektur des Hauses ist weder symbolisch noch narrativ, vielmehr sucht sie ihre Bedeutung durch die abstrakte Form und dynamische Bewegung, um mit der Umgebung, dem Licht, dem Meer und den Stimmungen zu arbeiten, die diesen magischen Ort am Golf umfangen. Das Fließende, Bewegte der Oberfläche bestimmt das einzigartige Äußere des Gebäudes, ohne es durch eine übertriebene Geste von einer vorgegebenen Bedeutung oder Assoziation abhängig zu machen. Vielmehr verleihen die angewendeten mathematischen Operationen, ähnlich wie bei Arabesken oder abstrakter islamischer Kalligrafie, dem Gebäude seine Eleganz und Musikalität.« Die Gestaltung des für Luxuswohnungen gedachten Turms basiert auch auf der fließenden, computergenerierten Formensprache des New Yorker Architekturbüros. Nur wenige der in großer Zahl in den Vereinigten Arabischen Emiraten errichteten Gebäude weisen eine vergleichbare architektonische Qualität auf. Ein Zeichen der Zeit, das sicher dafür spricht, dass Abu Dhabi das Interesse an einer Verbesserung der gestalterischen Qualität seiner Neubauten bemerkt hat.

Cette tour de 50 niveaux devrait être le plus haut immeuble de l'aménagement de la zone d'Al Raha Beach. Selon Hani Rashid : « L'architecture de la tour n'est ni symbolique ni narrative, mais cherche plutôt son sens dans une représentation abstraite de forme et de mouvement dynamique en échange avec l'environnement, la lumière, la mer et l'atmosphère qui enveloppent ce lieu magique en bordure du Golfe Arabe. Le flux et le mouvement qu'exprime la surface lui permettent d'accéder à un statut iconique, sans être pour autant un geste ostentatoire ni s'appuyer sur un sens ou une association d'idées attendues. Les processus mathématiques utilisés, proches de ceux illustrés par les arabesques ou la calligraphie islamique abstraite, donnent à l'immeuble son élégance et sa musicalité. » Destiné à des appartements de luxe, ce projet s'inspire également du style coulant issu de la conception assistée par ordinateur qui est celui de ces architectes new-yorkais. Malgré le grand nombre d'immeubles érigés dans les EAU, peu d'entre eux possèdent une qualité architecturale aussi évocatrice, signe des temps, et Abu Dhabi semble avoir compris l'intérêt d'améliorer la qualité de ses nouvelles constructions.

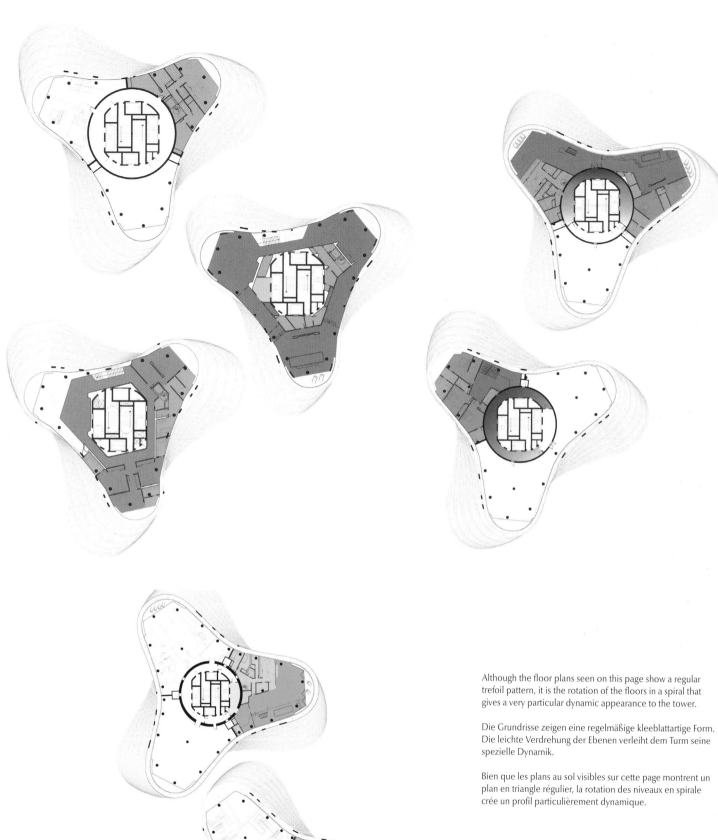

Although the floor plans seen on this page show a regular trefoil pattern, it is the rotation of the floors in a spiral that gives a very particular dynamic appearance to the tower.

Die Grundrisse zeigen eine regelmäßige kleeblattartige Form. Die leichte Verdrehung der Ebenen verleiht dem Turm seine spezielle Dynamik.

Bien que les plans au sol visibles sur cette page montrent un plan en triangle régulier, la rotation des niveaux en spirale crée un profil particulièrement dynamique.

Increasingly involved in interiors and design, Asymptote has carried the exterior appearance of the building into the surprising, flowing interiors.

Asymptote ist verstärkt auch im Bereich Design und Innenarchitektur tätig. Die äußere Gestaltung des Gebäudes setzt sich in den einzigartigen, fließenden Innenräumen fort.

De plus en plus impliqué dans l'architecture intérieure et le design, Asymptote a décliné le style extérieur du bâtiment dans des intérieurs fluides et surprenants.

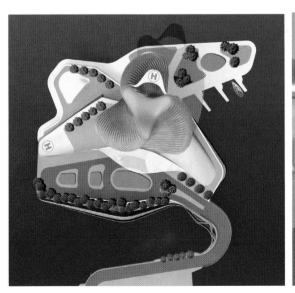

ATKINS

WS ATKINS & PARTNERS OVERSEAS
P. O. Box 5620
Dubai
United Arab Emirates

Tel: +971 4 405 9300
Fax: +971 4 405 9301
e-mail: office.dubai@atkinsglobal.com
Web: www.atkins-me.com

ATKINS is the largest engineering consultancy in the UK, and the world's third-largest global design firm. With a staff of 17 000, they are the fourth-largest employer of civil and structural staff in the world, and the second-biggest employer of architects in the UK (167). Their Middle Eastern affiliate is currently working on the DSEC Commercial Tower, the Al Shafar Development (all in Dubai), and the spectacular Trump International Hotel and Tower, The Palm Jumeirah, a double 60-story skyscraper that forms a single volume in its upper levels. The architect of the Burj Al Arab hotel was Tom Wright, born in 1957, a graduate of London's Kingston University (formerly known as Kingston Polytechnic) in 1982. Wright joined Marshall Haines and Barrow that later became Lester Drew Haines Barrow (LDHB). The company was acquired by WS Atkins in 1991 to form Atkins Lester Drew. In 1993, Wright moved to Dubai to head up the multidisciplinary design team and to work on the Chicago Beach Resort Development on the shores of the Arabian Gulf. This development became Atkins' signature design comprising the Jumeirah Beach Hotel, the Wild Wadi Aqua Park and the Burj Al Arab Hotel. Wright returned to the UK in 1998 to form the national working group to control Atkins' offices throughout the country. He became Head of Architecture in 2000 and subsequently Design Director for Design Environment and Engineering in 2001. His current and past projects include: the design of the Burj Al Arab, published here; the Durrat Al Bahrain, Bahrain; Al Rajhi Tower, Riyadh, Saudi Arabia; Millennium Residence, Bangkok, Thailand; Al Diyafa Hotel and Residence Tower, Mecca, Saudi Arabia; and Pantai Mutiara, Jakarta Bay Arch Hotel, Jakarta, Indonesia. Wright is currently involved in the Lake Side Resort in Tunis. Shaun Killa was born in 1970, in Cape Town, South Africa, and received his Bachelor of Architectural Studies and Bachelor in Architecture degrees from the University of Cape Town. He worked for Munnick Visser and Stefan Antoni Architects before moving to Dubai and joining Atkins in 1998 as part of the team on the Burj Al Arab. In 2000 he became Head of Architecture and later Design Director for Atkins Dubai. He has won several commissions, such as the Dubai Flower Centre (2001–05), the Millennium Tower (2003–06), and Al Mas Tower (2005–08), which assisted in expanding the office from 60 to over 500 staff. He also has been the Principal Architect for the Bahrain World Trade Center, Manama, Bahrain (2003–07).

BURJ AL ARAB
DUBAI, UAE
1994-'99

HEIGHT: 321 m
CLIENT: Jumeirah
COST: not disclosed

Located 15 kilometers south of the city of Dubai, the Burj Al Arab is part of the Jumeirah Beach Resort that also includes the Jumeirah Beach Hotel and Wild Wadi Water Park. Built on a man-made island set 280 meters offshore in the Arabian Gulf, at a height of 321 meters the building is the tallest hotel building in the world. The iconic sail shape of the structure has led it to be photographed frequently and it has in some sense become the symbol of the rapid and spectacular development of Dubai. The unusual location of the building led to the necessity of driving piles 40 meters into the seabed. The sail façade features a double-skinned, Teflon-coated, woven glass-fiber screen. Despite its substantial height, the Burj Al Arab is 28 duplex stories high. It is topped by a helipad. The Burj Al Arab contains 202 duplex suites ranging from 170 square meters to 780 square meters in size. A panoramic 140-seat restaurant, the Al Muntaha (meaning "ultimate" or "highest" in Arabic), is set 200 meters above the sea. The core of the hotel is an open 180-meter atrium, apparently the world's highest. A number of water features, such as the 20 000-liter Ellipse waterfall on the entry roundabout, or "sudden bursts of water shooting 42 meters upwards" in the atrium, contribute to the overall effect of extravagance. Thirty different types of marble cover a total of 24 000 square meters in the hotel, and no less than 8000 square meters of 22-carat gold leaf were used in the interior designs. The luxury of the design and the nature of its accommodations originally led its promoters to bill it as the world's first (and only) "seven star hotel."

Das Hotel Burj al-Arab 15 km südlich von Dubai ist Teil des Jumeirah Beach Resort, zu dem auch das Jumeirah Beach Hotel und der Wild Wadi Water Park gehören. Es wurde auf einer 280 m weit in den Golf ragenden, künstlich angelegten Halbinsel errichtet. Mit seinen 321 m ist es das weltweit höchste Hotel. Seine markante, an ein geblähtes Segel erinnernde Silhouette macht es zu einem beliebten Fotomotiv; in gewisser Weise symbolisiert es Dubais schnelle und spektakuläre Entwicklung. Aufgrund seines ungewöhnlichen Standorts mussten Pfähle 40 m tief in den Meeresboden getrieben werden. Die konvex gewölbte Fassade besteht aus einer doppelschaligen, teflonbeschichteten Oberfläche aus gewebten Glasfasern. Trotz der beachtlichen Höhe hat das Burj al-Arab nur 28 Doppelgeschosse. An seiner Spitze befindet sich ein Hubschrauberlandeplatz. Das Hotel verfügt über 202 Doppelsuiten mit 170 m² bis 780 m² Fläche. Das Panoramarestaurant Al-Muntaha

(arabisch für »das Ultimative« oder »das Höchste«) für 140 Gäste schwebt 200 m über dem Meeresspiegel. Die Mitte des Gebäudes bildet ein 180 m hohes Atrium, wohl das höchste der Welt. Eine Reihe von Wasserspielen, etwa der »Ellipse« getaufte Wasserfall in der Mitte der runden Eingangsvorfahrt, bei dem 20 000 l Wasser in die Tiefe stürzen, oder im Atrium angeordnete »Fontänen, die plötzlich 42 m hoch schießen« tragen zum allgemeinen Eindruck der Extravaganz bei. Insgesamt sind 24 000 m² Fläche mit 30 verschiedenen Marmorarten belegt und nicht weniger als 8000 m² Fläche in den Innenräumen mit 22-karätigem Blattgold ausgestattet. Aufgrund der verschwenderischen Ausstattung und der luxuriösen Zimmer sollte das Burj al-Arab ursprünglich als weltweit erstes (und einziges) Sieben-Sterne-Hotel beworben werden.

Situé à 15 kilomètres au sud de la ville de Dubaï, la Burj Al Arab fait partie du Jumeirah Beach Resort qui comprend également le Jumeirah Beach Hotel et le Wild Wadi Water Park. Construit sur une île artificielle éloignée de 280 m seulement de la côte du Golfe Arabe et culminant à 321 m, cet hôtel est le plus haut du monde. Sa forme de voile si identifiable en a fait un sujet favori des photographes et il est devenu, en un sens, le symbole du développement rapide et spectaculaire de Dubaï. Sa localisation particulière a entraîné la pose de pieux de 40 m de haut reposant sur le fond de la mer. La façade est composée d'un écran de fibre de verre tissée, enduite de téflon à double peau. Malgré son impressionnante hauteur, l'hôtel, surmonté d'une plate-forme pour hélicoptères, ne compte que 28 double-niveaux. Il contient 202 suites en duplex, chacune de 170 à 780 m². Un restaurant panoramique de 140 couverts, l'Al Muntaha (l'ultime ou le plus haut, en arabe) a été aménagé à 200 m au-dessus du niveau de la mer. La cour est un atrium de 180 m de haut, sans doute le plus élevé du monde. Un certain nombre de jeux d'eau, comme la cascade Ellipse de 20 000 litres de débit au rond-point de l'entrée, là où « de brusques geysers jaillissent à 42 m » dans l'atrium, contribuent à donner une impression d'extravagance mise en scène. Trente variétés de marbres différents recouvrent 24 000 m² et pas moins de 8000 m² de feuilles d'or de 22 carats ont été utilisés à la décoration. Le luxe de ce projet et la nature de ses aménagements expliquent que ses promoteurs l'annonçaient au départ comme le premier (et seul) hôtel « sept étoiles » au monde.

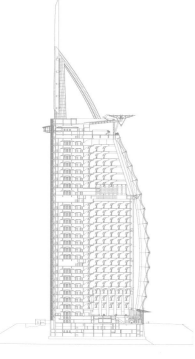

Set off the coast, the hotel retains a spectacular presence along the shoreline despite the rapid development of other resorts and apartment buildings along the entire sea front nearby.

Entlang des Küstenabschnitts werden in rasantem Tempo Ferienanlagen und Apartmenthochhäuser errichtet. Trotzdem bleibt die spektakuläre Präsenz des vor der Küste stehenden Hotels erhalten.

Détaché de la côte, l'hôtel affirme sa présence spectaculaire le long du rivage malgré le développement rapide d'autres ensembles hôteliers et résidentiels voisins sur le front de mer.

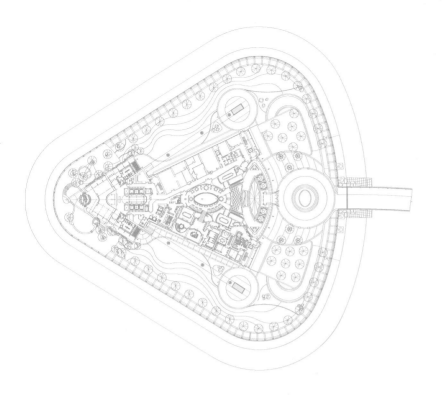

One of the main features of the interior of the hotel is the soaring lobby with its fountain and vertiginous balconies. Cost was clearly no object in the selection of the materials, with an interior design that corresponds to regional taste.

Ein wesentliches räumliches Element des Hotels ist die turmhohe Lobby mit einem Springbrunnen und den schwindelerregenden Galerien. Bei der Auswahl der Materialien spielten die Kosten offensichtlich keine Rolle; die Gestaltung der Innenräume trägt dem landestypischen Geschmack Rechnung.

L'une des principales caractéristiques de l'hôtel est son hall d'accueil gigantesque, décoré d'une fontaine, sur lequel donnent de vertigineux balcons. Le coût n'était à l'évidence pas un obstacle au choix des matériaux. Le style correspond au goût régional.

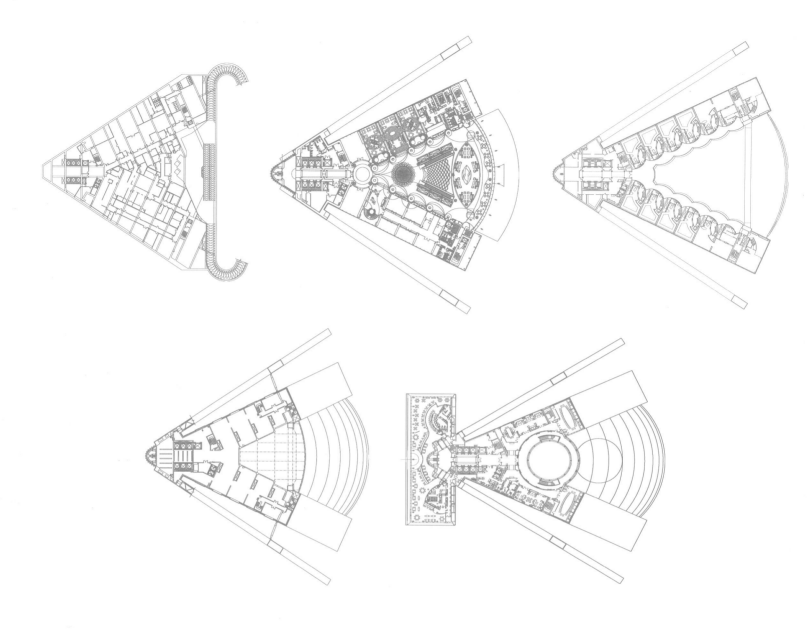

The atrium of the hotel, here somewhat deformed
by the camera's lens, corresponds to the central element
seen in the plans above.

Das Atrium, hier durch die Kameralinse etwas
verzerrt, entspricht dem Element in der Mitte der Grundrisse.

L'atrium de l'hôtel, ici légèrement déformé par l'objectif,
correspond à l'élément central figurant sur le plan ci-dessus.

BAHRAIN WORLD TRADE CENTER
MANAMA, BAHRAIN
2003 - 07

AREA: 88 617 m²
HEIGHT: 240 m
CLIENT: not disclosed
COST: not disclosed

This design features the first large-scale integration of wind turbines in a building. Part of a master plan to update an existing hotel and shopping mall set on a prestigious site near the Arabian Gulf, the double 50-story structure was inspired in part by traditional Arabian wind towers. Three 29-meter wind turbines are suspended between the towers, and, indeed, the very shape of the buildings is related to this function. The architects write, "Vertically, the sculpting of the towers is also a function of airflow dynamics. As they taper upwards, their aerofoil sections reduce. This effect when combined with the increasing velocity of the onshore breeze at increasing heights, creates a near equal regime of wind velocity on each of the three turbines." The architects also explain that they were inspired by the form of the sail in their quest to "harness the consistent onshore breezes." Their use of fixed turbines, only able to operate with wind coming onshore, was validated through extensive wind tunnel testing. These tests showed that the tapering form of the buildings will increase wind speed on the turbines by as much as 30 %. Given the reliance of the region on the production of fossil fuels, this very visible integration of wind power has a symbolic meaning as well. With the knowledge that the attempted integration of wind turbines into buildings has failed for reasons of the costs related to custom designs, Atkins worked with existing "conventional" technologies and set out to design a building that would readily integrate the turbines. A number of other significant features in the overall building design are intended to reduce the carbon emissions of the structures. The towers are integrated on top of a three-story podium and basement that accommodate a new shopping center, restaurants, business centers, and car parking. The towers each contain 34 stories of office space, and a viewing deck is located on the 42nd floor.

Das Bahrain World Trade Center ist das erste Gebäude, das in großem Maßstab Windräder integriert. Es ist Bestandteil eines Masterplans zur Modernisierung eines vorhandenen Hotels und Einkaufszentrums in prominenter Lage in der Nähe des Golfes. Inspiriert wurden die 50-geschossigen Zwillingstürme auch von den traditionellen arabischen Windtürmen. Drei Windräder mit einem Durchmesser von jeweils 29 m schweben zwischen den Türmen, deren Form in Zusammenhang mit den Windrädern steht. Die Architekten schreiben: »Die Höhenentwicklung der Türme ergibt sich auch aus den Luftströmungen. Durch ihre Verjüngung reduziert sich der Luftwiderstand der Türme kontinuierlich in der Höhe. In Verbindung mit der höheren Windgeschwindigkeit in den höheren Bereichen sorgt dies für eine annähernd gleichmäßige Windlast auf die drei Windräder.« Die Architekten erläutern, dass bei ihren Bestrebungen, »den stetigen Küstenwind nutzbar zu machen« auch die Form eines Segels als Vorbild diente. Die Wirkungsweise der Windräder, die sich nur drehen können, wenn der Wind auflandig weht, wurde in zahlreichen Tests im Windkanal geprüft. Die Tests zeigten, dass die sich verjüngende Gebäu-deform die Windgeschwindigkeit im Bereich der Windräder um bis zu 30 % erhöht. In Anbetracht der Abhängigkeit der Region von fossilen Brennstoffen hat diese sehr sichtbare Integration der Windräder auch eine symbolische Bedeutung. Aufgrund der hohen Kosten für Spezialanfertigungen, die eine Verwendung von Windrädern in Gebäuden schon häufig verhindert haben, arbeitete WS Atkins mit konventionellen Technologien und entwarf einen Bau, der eine problemlose Integration der Windräder erlaubt. Eine Reihe weiterer konzeptioneller Maßnahmen soll den Kohlendioxidausstoß beim Betrieb der Gebäude senken. Die Türme stehen auf einem gemeinsamen dreigeschossigen Unterbau mit Kellergeschoss, in dem ein neues Einkaufszentrum, Restaurants, Businessbereiche und Parkplätze untergebracht sind. Jeder Turm hat 34 Bürogeschosse, eine Aussichtsplattform befindet sich im 42. Geschoss.

Ce projet a bénéficié du premier essai d'intégration de turbines à vent de grandes dimensions dans un immeuble. Composante du plan de rénovation d'une zone comprenant déjà un hôtel et un centre commercial, implantée sur un site prestigieux en bordure du Golfe, ce double immeuble de 50 niveaux s'inspire en partie des tours à vent arabes traditionnelles. Trois turbines de 29 m sont suspendues entre les deux parties du bâtiment dont la forme même exprime cette fonction. Pour les architectes : « Verticalement, les tours ont été sculptées en fonction de la dynamique des flux. Au fur et à mesure qu'elles s'effilent vers le haut, leurs sections transversales diminuent. Cet effet, combiné à la vitesse croissante de la brise du large au fur et à mesure que l'on prend de l'altitude, crée un régime de vitesse du vent quasi égal sur chacune des trois turbines. » Ils ont également été inspirés par la forme d'une voile pour tenter de « capter les vents de mer consistants ». Seules des turbines fixes pouvaient s'adapter à ce type de vents, comme l'ont montré des recherches approfondies menées en soufflerie. Ces tests ont prouvé que la forme effilée des tours permettrait d'accroître la vitesse du vent sur les turbines de près de 30 %. Si l'on considère que l'économie de la région repose encore sur l'exploitation de ressources fossiles, cette intégration très visible de celle de la force du vent présente une signification symbolique forte. De précédentes tentatives d'intégration d'éoliennes avaient échoué pour des raisons de coût de fabrication de modèles adaptés. Atkins a travaillé à partir de technologies « conventionnelles » existantes et a conçu un bâtiment qui intégrait ces turbines dès le départ. Un certain nombre d'autres équipements importants prévus également très en amont sont destinés à réduire les émissions de carbone. Les tours partent d'un podium de trois niveaux, en partie souterrain, qui regroupe un centre commercial, des restaurants, des centres d'affaires et des parkings. Chaque tour contient 34 étages de bureaux. Une plate-forme d'observation est installée au 42e niveau.

Interior drawings and a bird's eye view of the tower in its planned location, taking advantage of the nearby water to channel airflows through its central windmills.

Innenraumperspektiven und Vogelperspektive des Turms; die Nähe zum Wasser wird genutzt, um mit dem Wind vom Meer die zentral angeordneten Windräder anzutreiben.

Perspectives dessinées de l'intérieur et vue aérienne de la tour sur son site. Elle bénéficie de la présence immédiate de la mer qui oriente les vents vers les éoliennes.

The leaning, spiked appearance of the towers along the water, with their three large windmills suspended between the volumes. Below, a section of the lower levels.

Ansicht vom Meer mit den abgeschrägten, spitzen Türmen und den dazwischen schwebenden drei großen Windrädern; unten: Schnitt durch die unteren Geschosse.

Les tours effilées en pointe et leurs trois grandes éoliennes suspendues entre leurs volumes légèrement inclinés. En bas, coupe d'un des niveaux inférieurs.

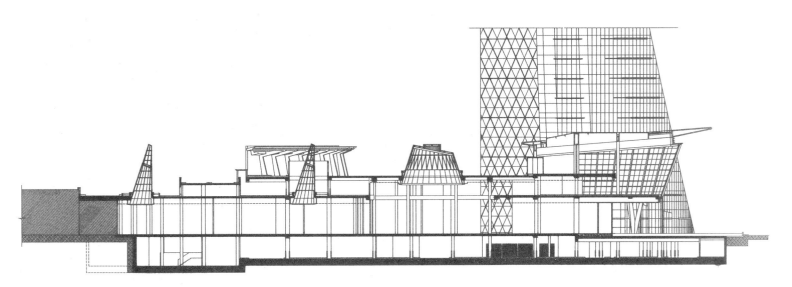

To the left, images of the project under construction.
Below, sections of the two towers.

Links: die Türme im Bau;
unten: Schnittzeichnungen der beiden Türme.

À gauche, images du projet en cours de construction.
Ci-dessous, coupes des deux tours.

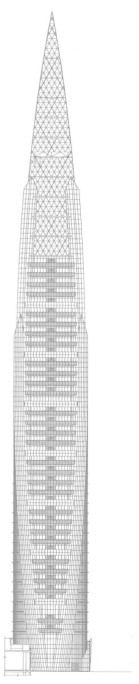

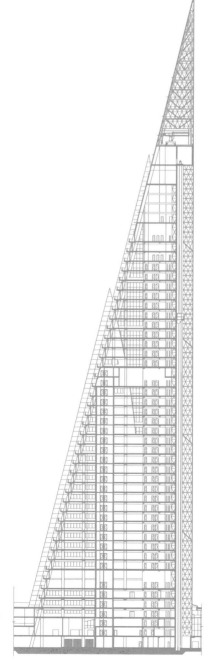

The perspective above, showing the windmills in place, is an unexpected combination of a futuristic architecture with a very ancient method of power generation, expressed of course in terms of sophisticated modern technology.

Die Perspektive oben zeigt die installierten Windräder. Auf überraschende Weise verbinden sich futuristische Architektur und eine sehr alte Form der Energiegewinnung, die natürlich mithilfe anspruchsvoller moderner Technologie umgesetzt wird.

La perspective ci-dessus montre les turbines à vent en place, combinaison surprenante d'une architecture futuriste et d'une très ancienne méthode de production d'énergie exprimée dans une technologie contemporaine.

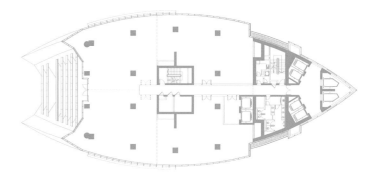

BEHNISCH ARCHITECTS

BEHNISCH ARCHITECTS
Rotebühlstr. 163A
70 190 Stuttgart
Germany

Tel: +49 711 607 720
Fax: +49 711 607 7299
e-mail: buero@behnisch.com
Web: www.behnisch.com

Born in 1922 in Dresden, **GUNTER BEHNISCH** grew up in Dresden and in Chemnitz. He studied architecture from 1947 to 1951 at the Technical University of Stuttgart (Dipl.-Ing.) before setting up his own office in 1952. In 1966, he created the firm of Behnisch & Partner, and from 1967 to 1987 he was a Professor for Design, Industrial Buildings and Planning, and Director of the Institute for Building Standardization at the Technical University, Darmstadt. In 1989, he established a city office in Stuttgart, which has now become Behnisch, Behnisch & Partner. **STEFAN BEHNISCH** was born in 1957 in Stuttgart. He studied philosophy at the Philosophische Hochschule der Jesuiten, Munich (1976–79), economics at the Ludwig-Maximilians University, Munich, and architecture at the University of Karlsruhe (1979–89). He worked at Stephen Woolley & Associates (Venice, CA, 1984–85), and has been principal partner of Behnisch Architects (until 2005 Behnisch, Behnisch & Partner) since 1989. This practice, which was originally founded as a branch office of Günter Behnisch's practice Behnisch & Partner, has planned and realised projects in the Netherlands, the USA, Canada, France, Italy, and, of course, Germany. Partners in Behnisch Architects are David Cook, born 1966 in Manchester, and Martin Haas, born 1967 in Waldshut.

ACROPOLIS UNIVERSE

DUBAI, UAE
2004-05

SITE AREA: 86 ha
CLIENT: WCP Group, Glenview, CA, US
ARCHITECT AND GENERAL PLANNER: Behnisch Architects
ENVIRONMENTAL CONSULTANCY: TranssolarKlima Engineering

This project, or rather concept study, which won an Architectural Review/Cityscape Award in 2005, was originally planned for a site in Las Vegas under the title "Senscity Paradise Universe." It combines a game arcade, theatre, auditoria, restaurants, public gardens, exhibition spaces, and playgrounds, forming "a unique experience of a new, artificial landscape." Rather than creating traditional buildings, the architects sought to design "elements firmly embedded in the landscape. including a large artificial lake and extensive vegetation. A series of 37-meter-high, 91-meter-wide "flower-like" structures were designed to provide shade and cool air. As they write, "A primary objective of the project is to create a leisure park for families that also serves as a large-scale inhabitable educational tool capable of demonstrating nature and natural laws. Visitors will be able to directly experience how the forces of the inhospitable local climate—sun, wind, and extreme temperature ranges—can, through a progressive, sustainable design approach, be tempered to benefit the immediate microclimate, creating an oasis in the midst of the desert. Reduced consumption of non-renewable energy will be an essential element of the design concept." Although the sites in Las Vegas and Dubai presented different weather conditions, the essential environmental effects created by the use of water and air pumped through the "leaf" forms and air flow through the structures and the park's "valley" configuration remained valid in Dubai. The goal of the park was essentially to show how contemporary technology can extend the usual four-month period of comfortable weather conditions typical of desert climates.

Das Projekt, oder vielmehr die Konzeptstudie, wurde ursprünglich unter dem Namen Senscity Paradise Universe für einen Standort in Las Vegas entwickelt und 2005 mit dem Architectural Review/Cityscape Award ausgezeichnet. Der Themenpark umfasst eine Arkade mit Spielangeboten, ein Theater, mehrere Auditorien, Restaurants, öffentliche Gärten, Ausstellungsflächen sowie Spielplätze und bietet »das einzigartige Erlebnis einer neuen, künstlich angelegten Landschaft«. Den Architekten ging es weniger darum, Gebäude im traditionellen Sinn zu schaffen, vielmehr wollten sie Elemente entwerfen »die sehr eng mit ihrer Umgebung verbunden sind«. Dazu gehören ein großer künstlicher See und eine intensive Begrünung. 37 m hohe blumenartige Konstruktionen, 91 m im Durchmesser, spenden Schatten und erzeugen einen kühlenden Wind. Die Architekten erläutern: »Ein wesentliches Entwurfsziel besteht darin, einen Freizeitpark für Familien zu schaffen, der auch als betretbares, großmaßstäbliches Lerninstrument dient, das die Natur und die Gesetze der Natur darstellt. Besucher können hier direkt er-

leben, wie die Kräfte des unwirtlichen Klimas – Sonne, Wind und Temperaturextreme – durch einen innovativen und nachhaltigen Ansatz gebändigt werden können, der zur Verbesserung des Mikroklimas führt und eine Oase mitten in der Wüste entstehen lässt. Die Einsparung nicht erneuerbarer Energie ist ein zentrales Element des Entwurfskonzepts.« Auch wenn Las Vegas und Dubai unterschiedliche klimatische Bedingungen aufweisen, sind die Auswirkungen der Maßnahmen auf die Umwelt im Wesentlichen die gleichen: Durch die »Blätter« werden Wasser und Luft gepumpt, der Luftstrom durch die Konstruktion in Verbindung mit der Topografie des Parks in Form eines Tals erzeugt eine kühlende Luftbewegung. Das übergeordnete Ziel des Entwurfs bestand darin, zu zeigen, wie mithilfe moderner Technologie die normalerweise viermonatige Periode, während der in der Wüste angenehme klimatische Bedingungen herrschen, verlängert werden kann.

Ce projet, ou plutôt cette étude de concept, qui a remporté le Prix Architectural Review/Cityscape en 2005, était prévu à l'origine pour un terrain de Las Vegas et portait le titre de « Senscity Paradise Universe ». Il associe une salle de jeux, un théâtre, des auditoriums, des restaurants, des jardins publics, des espaces d'expositions et des terrains de jeux, le tout offrant « une expérience unique de nouveau paysage artificiel ». Plutôt que de créer des immeubles traditionnels, les architectes ont cherché à concevoir « des éléments fermement incrustés dans le paysage, dont un grand lac artificiel et une abondante végétation. Une suite de constructions de 37 m de haut et 91 m de large, en « forme de fleurs », a été dessinée pour fournir de l'ombre et rafraîchir l'air ». L'un des objectifs premiers du projet est de créer un parc de loisirs pour familles, qui soit également un outil éducatif habitable à grande échelle, capable d'illustrer la nature et ses lois. Les visiteurs pourront directement expérimenter la façon dont les forces caractéristiques d'un climat local hostile - soleil, vent et températures extrêmes - peuvent, grâce à une approche progressiste du développement durable, être tempérées pour obtenir un microclimat, en créant une oasis au milieu du désert. La réduction de la consommation d'énergies non renouvelables sera un élément essentiel de ce projet. » Bien que les sites de Las Vegas et de Dubaï présentent des conditions climatiques différentes, les effets environnementaux de base — créés par l'eau et l'air pompés par les formes en « feuilles » et le flux d'air généré par les constructions — et la configuration du parc en « vallée » restent valides en bordure du Golfe. L'objectif de ce lieu est essentiellement de montrer comment la technologie contemporaine peut servir à allonger la période des quatre mois de climat agréable en environnement désertique.

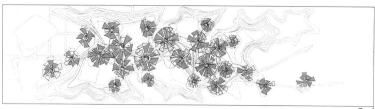

Roof

Architectural Elements

Main Concourse

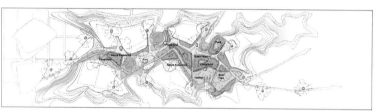

Green Elements

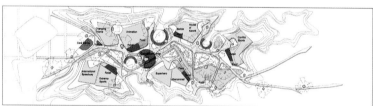

Facilities

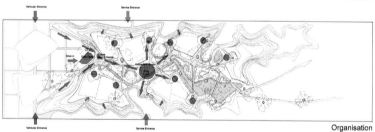

Organisation

Landscape

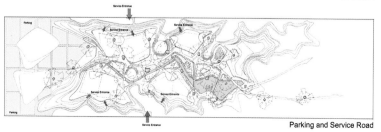

Parking and Service Road

Plans divide the complex into its constituent elements such as roads, green areas or architecture. The overall impression is one of an organic design quite distant from more familiar modernist plans.

Verschiedene Diagramme zeigen das Projekt und seine Elemente, z. B. Straßen, Grünflächen und überbaute Flächen. Der Gesamteindruck ist der eines organischen Entwurfs, der sich erheblich von gängigen funktionalistischen Planungen unterscheidet.

Plans directeur du complexe répartis en divers éléments : routes, espaces verts, constructions. L'impression générale donnée est celle d'une composition organique assez éloignée des propositions modernistes habituelles.

Although this project is not currently advancing, it represents one of the few real efforts in the region to respond to the difficult climatic conditions where daytime temperatures can reach up to 50° in summer.

Das Projekt wird derzeit nicht weiter verfolgt. Dabei ist es einer der wenigen ernst gemeinten Versuche, auf die schwierigen klimatischen Bedingungen vor Ort zu reagieren; die Tagestemperaturen können hier im Sommer 50°C erreichen.

Bien que ce projet soit pour l'instant arrêté, il représente un des rares efforts régionaux concrets de réponse à des conditions climatiques difficiles où la température diurne peut dépasser 50°C en été.

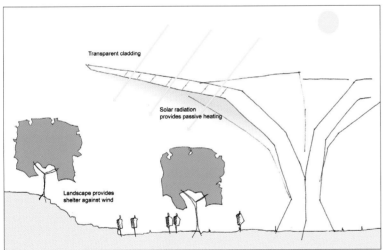

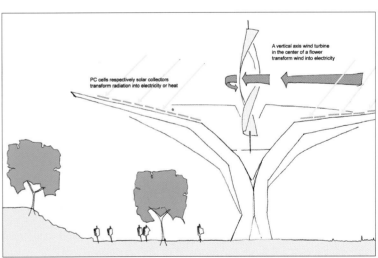

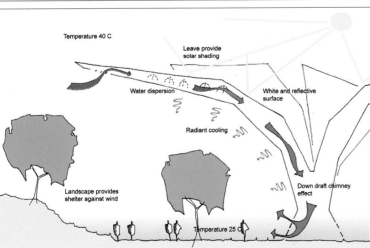

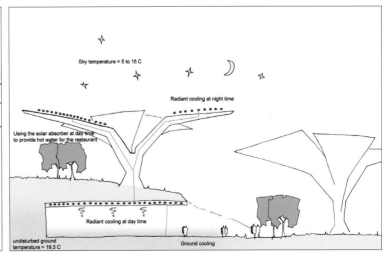

6

FRANK O. GEHRY

GEHRY PARTNERS, LLP
12541 Beatrice Street
Los Angeles, CA 90066
United States

Tel: +1 310 482 3000
Fax: +1 310 482 3006

Born in Toronto, Canada, in 1929, **FRANK GEHRY** received his Bachelor of Architecture degree from the University of Southern California in 1954, and at Harvard (1956-57). Principal of Frank O. Gehry and Associates, Inc., Los Angeles, since 1962, he received the Pritzker Prize in 1989. Some of his notable projects are the Loyola Law School, Los Angeles (1981–84); the Norton Residence, Venice, California (1982–1984); California Aerospace Museum, Los Angeles (1982–84); Schnabel Residence, Brentwood (1986–89); Festival Disney, Marne-la-Vallée, France (1989–92); Guggenheim Museum, Bilbao, Spain (1991–97); Experience Music Project, Seattle, Washington (1995–2000); and the unbuilt Guggenheim Museum, New York (1998–). Recent completed work includes the DG Bank Headquarters, Berlin, Germany (2000); Fisher Center for the Performing Arts at Bard College, Annandale-on-Hudson, New York (2003); Walt Disney Concert Hall, Los Angeles (2003); and the Massachusetts Institute of Technology Stata Complex, Cambridge, Massachusetts (2004). Recent and current work includes the Hotel Marques de Riscal, Elciego, Spain (2003–06); Ohr-O'Keefe Museums, Biloxi, Mississippi; King Alfred Leisure Centre, Brighton & Hove, United Kingdom; InterActiveCorp Headquarters, New York; Atlantic Yards, Brooklyn, New York; New World Symphony, Miami, Florida; and the Theatre for a New Audience, Brooklyn, New York.

GUGGENHEIM ABU DHABI
ABU DHABI, UAE
2006 -

AREA: 30 000 m²
EXHIBITION SPACE: 12 000 m²
CLIENT: Tourism Development
and Investment Company of Abu Dhabi (TDIC),
Solomon R. Guggenheim Foundation
COST: not disclosed

Frank Gehry's collaboration with the Guggenheim goes back to the Guggenheim Bilbao (Bilbao, Spain, 1991–97) and beyond. When he announced the project on January 31, 2007, Gehry emphasized that in his discussions with Thomas Krens of the Guggenheim they had agreed that the Abu Dhabi site required a different approach than would any other location. The architect stated, "We started with a very basic plan organization. The center core galleries were laid out forming a courtyard. Those galleries were of various heights and sizes, and placed one on top of another to create four floors. These galleries will be more classical contemporary galleries, completely air-conditioned, with skylights where possible, and a sophisticated lighting system. The next ring of galleries surrounding that core then radiating out of the center will be larger galleries in a variety of shapes and less formally constructed. The third ring is for larger galleries, built more like raw industrial space with exposed lighting and systems. They would be less finished. These galleries would be attractive as spawning homes for a new scale of contemporary art – art that would be, perhaps, made on-site and would be of a scale that could not be achieved in other museums around the world." The design, to be clad in stone, possibly with some color, is based in part on conical shaped tubes, and features such as water walls permit a natural cooling of the air in the outdoor spaces of the museum. Intended for contemporary art from around the world, the facility includes two large galleries for the Abu Dhabi Biennale that will be held in the Saadiyat Island cultural district.

Frank Gehrys Zusammenarbeit mit der Guggenheim Foundation reicht bis zum Guggenheim Bilbao (1991–97) und weiter zurück. Bei der Präsentation des Projekts am 31. Januar 2007 betonte Gehry, in seinen Gesprächen mit Thomas Krens, dem Direktor der Guggenheim Foundation, sei man übereingekommen, dass das Grundstück in Abu Dhabi einen anderen Entwurfsansatz erfordere als jeder andere Standort. Der Architekt erläuterte: »Wir begannen mit einem sehr einfachen Organisationsschema. Die wichtigsten Ausstellungsräume wurden um einen Hof herum angeordnet. Sie sind unterschiedlich hoch und groß und wurden übereinander gestapelt, um vier Ebenen zu schaffen. Diese Gallerien werden die eher klassisch-zeitgenössischen Ausstellungsräume, die zudem vollständig klimatisiert sein werden. Wo möglich, gibt es Oberlichter, darüber hinaus ein anspruchsvolles Beleuchtungskonzept. Der nächste Bereich, der den Kern strahlenförmig umgibt, wird aus größeren Ausstellungsräumen bestehen. Diese Räume werden unter-schiedlich geformt und weniger formal angelegt sein als jene im Zentrum des Museums. Der dritte, äußere Bereich ist ebenfalls für größere Ausstellungsräume vorgesehen, die eher den Charakter roher, unfertiger Industrieräume haben sollen. Belichtungs- und Versorgungssysteme werden hier sichtbar belassen. Diese Räume erlauben dann – möglicherweise direkt an diesem Ort – die Schaffung zeitgenössischer Kunst in einem neuen Maßstab. Dies wäre in den Museen, wie sie derzeit weltweit organisiert sind, nicht möglich.« Die Fassaden des Museums sollen aus Stein, eventuell mit etwas Farbe, bestehen. Einige Volumen sind kegelartig geformt. Die Kühlung der Außenräume zwischen den einzelnen Baukörpern erfolgt auf natürliche Weise, z. B. durch Wasserwände. In dem Museum soll zeitgenössische Kunst aus allen Teilen der Welt gezeigt werden. Zwei große Ausstellungsräume stehen der Abu Dhabi Biennale, die im Kulturdistrikt auf Saadiyat stattfinden soll, zur Verfügung.

La collaboration de Frank Gehry avec la Fondation Guggenheim remonte aux plans du musée de Bilbao (Espagne, 1991–97) et même au-delà. Lorsqu'il annonça ce nouveau projet le 31 janvier 2007, Gehry fit remarquer qu'il avait été décidé, lors des discussions avec Thomas Krens de la Fondation Guggenheim, que le site d'Abu Dhabi demanderait une approche différente de ce qui avait été fait par ailleurs : « Nous avons commencé par un plan d'organisation très basique. Les galeries du noyau central sont disposées de façon à former une cour. Elles sont de hauteurs et de dimensions variées et superposées sur quatre niveaux. Ce sont des galeries contemporaines classiques, entièrement climatisées, dotées de verrières zénithales lorsque c'est possible, et d'un système d'éclairage sophistiqué. L'anneau de galeries qui entoure ce premier dispositif part du centre et abritera des volumes plus vastes. Elles pourront prendre diverses formes moins conventionnelles que les précédentes. Le troisième anneau du plan sera consacré aux plus grandes galeries, davantage conçues comme des espaces industriels bruts dotés de systèmes techniques et d'éclairage apparents. » Le projet repose en partie sur des tubes coniques et possède des équipements spécifiques comme des murs d'eau qui permettront le rafraîchissement naturel de l'air dans les zones extérieures. L'ensemble sera habillé de pierre, avec, peut-être, quelques touches de couleur. Ce musée prévu pour accueillir des œuvres d'art contemporain international comptera également deux vastes galeries destinées à la Biennale d'Abu Dhabi qui se tiendra dans le quartier culturel de l'île de Saadiyat.

7

GENSLER

GENSLER
Roman House, Wood Street
London EC2Y 5BA
United Kingdom

Tel: +44 20 73 30 96 00
Fax: +44 20 73 30 96 30
e-mail: europe@gensler.com
Web: www.gensler.com

GENSLER was founded in 1966 by Art Gensler, Jim Follett, and Drue Gensler in San Francisco. The firm today has offices in 30 cities and has over 2800 employees. They describe themselves as a "global design consultancy." More specifically, they are involved in strategic consulting, master planning and urban design, architecture, landscape architecture, interior design, building design consultation, entail architecture/design and rollout, product strategy/design, brand strategy and design, graphic/signage design, facility management support, and information management consultation. R. K. Steward, a Principal at Gensler, is the 2007 President of the American Institute of Architects, and the firm has made sustainable design one of its hallmarks. The London office was opened in 1988 and currently employs over 180 people. Recent projects include the new London Stock Exchange; Apple's first European flagship store; a campus for GCHQ (Government Communications Head-quarters); as well as extensive work in the Middle East. Chris Johnson is the Managing Principal of Gensler in London. He received his degrees in Architecture from the Birmingham School of Architecture (1981, 1984) and worked on both the Saadiyat Island and DIFC master plans. Johnson was also involved in The Gate building in Dubai and the Ritz Carlton Hotel, also located in the DIFC. Ian Mulcahey obtained his degrees in Urban Planning at the University of Westminster (1986, 1987). He worked on the DIFC master plan in schematic and detailed design production, and the production and coordination of architectural design information. José Sirera joined Gensler in 1994. He received degrees in Architecture (1987) and Economy (1987) from Tulane University in New Orleans. He worked on The Gate and Ritz Carlton projects in the DIFC, and also on the Light House Hotel & Apartments (Palm Jumeirah, Dubai) and the Qatar Petroleum Headquarters in Doha.

DUBAI INTERNATIONAL FINANCIAL CENTER (DIFC) MASTER PLAN

DUBAI, UAE 2001-'04

AREA: 1.85 million m²
SITE AREA: 45 ha
CLIENT: Dubai International Financial
Center Authority (DIFC)
COST: not disclosed

The brief given to the architects revolved around the intention of the government of Dubai to turn the city into a regional financial center. They were asked to lead the development of a master plan for a single complex of buildings with a total of 1.85 million square meters of floor space for a 45-hectare site. They explain, "The master plan provided a rigorous physical organization of buildings and spaces around integrated transport and utility infrastructure. The master plan is conceived as a series of distinct districts each with their own function and character but all connected to form one complete complex. The site had been designated a free trade zone and was, for regulatory purposes, independent of the local municipality. Gensler were required, therefore, to establish long-term planning and design guidelines to ensure the proper implementation of the project. The planning and design guidelines set a new standard in Dubai for the implementation of large-scale development projects." The first phase of the project is the 90 000-square-meter Gate Building, designed by Gensler. This "landmark" design updates the age-old typology of the arch of triumph seen from Rome to Napoleonic Paris. Indeed, the Gensler master plan called for a "triumphal promenade reminiscent of the Champs-Elysées in Pars." Clearly intended to be monumental, the Gate Building symbolizes the "DIFC's permanence and stability," and is located on the axis of the iconic Emirates Towers. The upper levels of the Gate Building house the offices of the Dubai International Financial Authority, while the podium houses retail space and parking.

Das den Architekten aufgegebene Programm basiert auf der Absicht der Regierung von Dubai, die Stadt zu einem internationalen Finanzzentrum zu machen. Das Büro wurde beauftragt, die Entwicklung eines Masterplans für einen Gebäudekomplex mit einer Gesamtfläche von 1,85 Millionen m² Geschossfläche auf einem 45 ha großen Grundstück zu leiten. Die Architekten erläutern: »Der Masterplan gibt die strenge Organisation der Gebäude und Räume um eine integrierte Transport- und Versorgungsinfrastruktur vor. Er sieht eine Abfolge von unterschiedlichen Bereichen vor, die alle eine bestimmte Funktion und einen eigenen Charakter haben, gleichwohl miteinander verbunden sind und einen vollständigen Gesamt-

komplex bilden. Das Gelände ist als Freihandelszone ausgewiesen und aus regulierungstechnischen Gründen unabhängig von der Stadtverwaltung. Um die korrekte Durchführung des Projektes zu garantieren, musste Gensler langfristige Planungs- und Entwurfsrichtlinien festlegen. Diese Richtlinien setzten in Dubai einen neuen Standard bei der Durchführung von Entwicklungsprojekten dieser Größenordnung.« Die erste Phase des Projekts bildet das von Gensler entworfene Gebäude The Gate mit insgesamt 90 000 m². Das neue Wahrzeichen interpretiert den jahrhundertealten Typus des Triumphbogens neu. The Gate, eindeutig als Monumentalbau konzipiert, symbolisiert die »Beständigkeit und Stabilität des DIFC« und steht in einer Achse mit den markanten Emirates Towers.

Suivant l'intention des autorités de Dubaï d'en faire un centre financier régional, les architectes proposaient le plan directeur d'un complexe d'immeubles de 1,85 million de m² sur un terrain de 45 ha. L'agence explique que « le plan directeur devait proposer une organisation physique rigoureuse des immeubles et des espaces liés autour d'une infrastructure intégrée de transports et de services. Ce plan a pris la forme d'une série de quartiers possédant chacun sa fonction et son caractère, mais connectés pour former un complexe global. Le site décrété zone franche était, pour des raisons réglementaires, indépendant de la municipalité. Gensler a donc reçu mission d'établir une planification à long terme, avec des règles de conception garantissant la mise en œuvre et instaurant de nouveaux standards de création de projets immobiliers à grande échelle à Dubaï. » La première phase de ce projet est le Gate Building de 90 000 m² conçu par Gensler. Cette réalisation « monumentale » reprend et modernise la très ancienne typologie de l'arc de triomphe à Rome ou à Paris. Le plan évoquait d'ailleurs « une promenade triomphale rappelant les Champs-Élysées ». Volontairement monumental, The Gate (la porte) symbolisant « la permanence et la stabilité du DIFL » est située dans l'axe des Emirates Towers, déjà considérées comme des icônes. L'immeuble accueillera les bureaux de l'Autorité financière internationale de Dubaï, des commerces et des parkings.

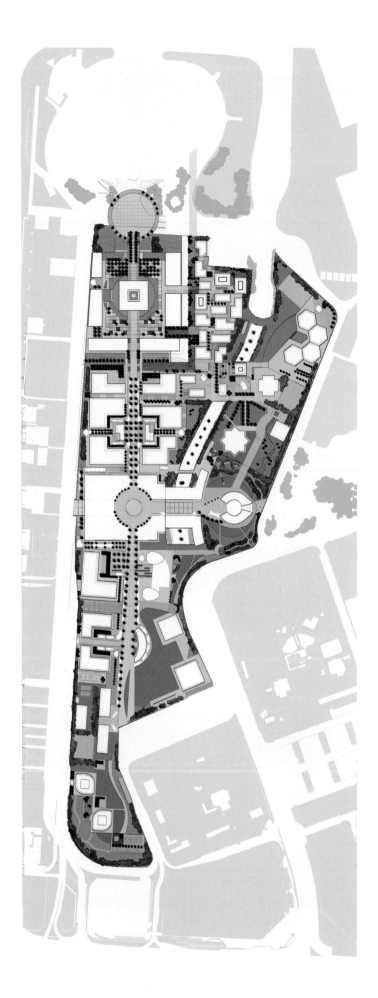

The overall master plan of the International Financial Center (left) with the Gate Building located at the top of the drawing.

Masterplan des International Financial Center (links) mit dem Gebäude The Gate am oberen Rand der Zeichnung.

Le plan directeur de l'International Finance Center (à gauche). The Gate est située en partie haute.

Recent images taken in the DIFC with the Gate Building visible to the left of the pictures. Upper right, a view through the opening of the Gate Building to the nearby Emirates Towers.

Vor Kurzem aufgenommene Bilder des DIFC; links im Bild The Gate; oben rechts: Blick durch The Gate auf die Emirates Towers.

De récentes images prises dans le DIFC. The Gate est visible à gauche. En haut à droite, une perspective à travers la porte vers les Emirates Towers situées à proximité.

BANK HEADQUARTERS DOHA, QATAR 2006 -

FLOOR AREA: 100 000 m²
CLIENT: not disclosed
COST: not disclosed

This unusual 500-meter tower intended for the capital of Qatar makes a distinct reference to Islamic tradition in spite of its radical form. As the architects explain, "The design concept for the bank headquarters embodies the Islamic belief that the earth and the universe are interconnected. The design draws its inspiration from the night sky and is a representation of the cosmos. Using computer-aided technology, the ancient two-dimensional Islamic geometric pattern is transformed into a modern building. The points of the constellation are joined in three dimensions and a new model for the bank of the future is created." Located near the city's tourist sites and the future Education City, the building is obviously meant to be iconic, or symbolic of the new directions of the Emirate and of its bank in this instance. A "large angular water feature" with a kinetic sculpture is planned for the plaza near the building on the south side. The theme of the cosmos is developed in numerous aspects of the design including landscape lighting intended to represent "the nebular and the galaxy." The tower itself is conceived as a link between the sea and the sky, with a bright light at its apex shining like "a new star over Qatar."

Der ungewöhnliche, 500 m hohe Turm, der in der Hauptstadt von Katar errichtet werden soll, weist trotz seiner radikalen Form starke Bezüge zur islamischen Tradition auf. Die Architekten erläutern: »Der Entwurf für die Bankzentrale bringt die islamische Vorstellung, dass die Erde und das Universum miteinander verbunden sind, zum Ausdruck. Inspiriert von dem nächtlichen Himmel, repräsentiert das Gebäude den Kosmos. Mithilfe von CAD-Technik wurde ein altes islamisches geometrisches Muster in ein modernes Gebäude übersetzt. Punkte des Musters wurden dreidimensional miteinander verbunden und ein Modell für ein Bankgebäude der Zukunft geschaffen.« Das Gebäude befindet sich in der Nähe der Touristenat-traktionen der Stadt und der zukünftigen Education City. Ganz offensichtlich soll es als Wahrzeichen oder als Symbol der neuen Ausrichtung des Emirats bzw. der Nationalbank von Katar fungieren. Eine »große, winklige Wasserfläche« mit einer kinetischen Skulptur ist auf einem Platz auf der Südseite des Gebäudes geplant. Das Thema des Kosmos wird auf verschiedene Weise interpretiert, u. a. durch die Beleuchtung der Umgebung, die »das Nebelartige und die Galaxie« repräsentieren soll. Der Turm selbst soll die Verbindung zwischen Meer und Himmel versinnbildlichen. An seiner Spitze leuchtet ein helles Licht als »neuer Stern über Katar«.

Cette étrange tour de 500 mètres de haut prévue pour la capitale du Qatar fait une référence précise à la tradition islamique en dépit de sa forme radicale. Comme l'expliquent les architectes : « Le concept du siège de la banque incarne la conviction islamique selon laquelle la terre et l'univers sont interconnectés. Le projet tire son inspiration du ciel nocturne et donne une représentation du cosmos. Des motifs géométriques islamiques bidimensionnels anciens sont adaptés à la construction moderne grâce à des technologies numériques. Les points de constellations sont reliés en trois dimensions et créent un nouveau modèle de banque du futur. » Situé près des principaux sites touristiques de la capitale et de la future « Ville de l'éducation », l'immeuble veut à l'évidence devenir une icône ou un symbole des nouvelles orientations de l'émirat et de sa banque. Un « vaste bassin anguleux » et une sculpture cinétique orneront la place au pied de la tour, côté sud. Le thème du cosmos se retrouve dans de nombreux aspects du projet, par exemple dans l'éclairage de son environnement qui devrait représenter « la nébuleuse et la galaxie ». La tour est conçue comme un lien entre la mer et le ciel. Un projecteur à son sommet brillera comme « une nouvelle étoile sur le Qatar ».

8

ZAHA HADID

ZAHA HADID
Studio 9
10 Bowling Green Lane
London EC1R OBQ
United Kingdom

Tel: +44 20 72 53 51 47
Fax: +44 20 72 51 83 22
e-mail: mail@zaha-hadid.com
Web: www.zaha-hadid.com

ZAHA HADID studied architecture at the Architectural Association in London (AA) beginning in 1972 and was awarded the Diploma Prize in 1977. She then became a partner of Rem Koolhaas in the Office for Metropolitan Architecture (OMA) and taught at the AA. She has also taught at Harvard, the University of Chicago, in Hamburg and at Columbia University in New York. Well-known for her paintings and drawings, she has had a substantial influence, despite having built relatively few buildings. She has completed the Vitra Fire Station, Weil-am-Rhein, Germany (1990–94); and exhibition designs such as that for "The Great Utopia", Solomon R. Guggenheim Museum, New York (1992). Significant competition entries include her design for the Cardiff Bay Opera House, Wales, UK (1994–96); the Habitable Bridge, London (1996); and the Luxembourg Philharmonic Hall (1997). More recently, Zaha Hadid has entered a phase of active construction with such projects as the Bergisel Ski Jump, Innsbruck, Austria (2001–02); Lois & Richard Rosenthal Center for Contemporary Art, Cincinnati, Ohio (1999–2003); Phaeno Science Center, Wolfsburg, Germany (2001–05); and Central Building of the BMW Assembly Plant in Leipzig, Germany (2005). She is working on the Price Tower Arts Center, Bartlesville, Oklahoma; Doha Tower, Doha, Qatar; and made a proposal for the 2012 Olympic Village, New York. In 2004, Zaha Hadid became the first woman to win the coveted Pritzker Prize. The Sheikh Zayed Bridge in Abu Dhabi is currently under construction and due for 2012 completion. The MAXXI Center of Contemporary Arts, Rome, Italy; the Architecture Foundation, London; University of Seville Library, Seville, Spain; and the Guangzhou Opera House, Guangzhou, China, are all due to be completed in 2008.

ABU DHABI PERFORMING ARTS CENTER
ABU DHABI, UAE
2007-12

CLIENT: Tourism Development and Investment
Company of Abu Dhabi (TDIC),
Solomon R. Guggenheim Foundation

This 62-meter-high building is intended to house a music hall, concert hall, opera house, drama theater, and a flexible theater. The combined seating capacity of the facility will be for 6300 people. This is one of the five cultural institutions being created by the Tourism Development and Investment Company of Abu Dhabi (TDIC), assisted by the Solomon R. Guggenheim Foundation. In 2004, the Abu Dhabi Tourism Authority (ADTA) asked Gensler to create a master plan for Saadiyat Island (Island of Happiness), a 27-square-kilometer natural island, into a "world-class, environmentally sensitive tourist destination." The centerpiece of this scheme is the 270-hectare cultural district, master planned by Skidmore, Owings & Merrill (SOM), where Tadao Ando, Jean Nouvel and Frank Gehry also have buildings planned. Zaha Hadid described the design of the Performing Arts Center as "a sculptural form that emerges from a linear intersection of pedestrian paths within the cultural district, gradually developing into a growing organism that sprouts a network of successive branches. As it winds through the site, the architecture increases in complexity, building up height and depth and achieving multiple summits in the bodies housing the performance spaces, which spring from the structure like fruits on a vine and face westward, toward the water." In fact, Zaha Hadid would seem to be justifiably enthusiastic about the development of the new cultural projects in Abu Dhabi. She states, "The plans for Saadiyat Island and the cultural district, envisioned and developed by the Abu Dhabi government, are, quite simply, extraordinary. When this comprehensive and inclusive vision is realized, it will set a standard for global culture that will resonate for decades to come."

Das 62 m hohe Gebäude soll einen Musiksaal, einen Konzertsaal, ein Opernhaus, einen klassischen Theatersaal und eine Mehrzweckbühne enthalten. Die Gesamtkapazität des Hauses liegt bei 6300 Plätzen. Hadids Bau ist einer von fünf Kulturbauten, die unter Leitung der Tourismusentwicklungsgesellschaft TDIC entstehen sollen und dabei von der Solomon R. Guggenheim Foundation unterstützt werden. 2004 beauftragte die Abu Dhabi Tourism Authority (ADTA) das Büro Gensler mit der Erstellung eines Masterplans für die Insel Saadiyat (»Insel des Glücks«), eine 27 km² große natürliche Insel, die in eine »umweltgerechte Touristenattraktion von Weltrang« verwandelt werden soll. Einen wesentlichen Teil der Insel nimmt der 270 ha große Kulturdistrikt ein, für den wiederum Skidmore, Owings & Merrill (SOM) den Masterplan erstellten. Neben Zaha Hadid planen hier Tadao Ando, Jean Nouvel und Frank Gehry Kulturbauten. Die Architektin beschreibt ihren Entwurf für das Zentrum für darstellende Künste als »eine skulpturale Form, die

sich aus der Kreuzung linearer Fußgängerwege innerhalb des Kulturdistrikts ergibt. Diese Form entwickelt sich zu einem wachsenden Organismus aus einem Geflecht von Verästelungen. Das Gebäude windet sich über das Grundstück und nimmt an Komplexität, Höhe und Tiefe zu und erreicht in den Veranstaltungssälen seine räumlichen Höhepunkte. Die Säle, die dem Bau wie Trauben einem Rebstock entspringen, sind nach Westen, zum Wasser, ausgerichtet.« Es scheint, als wäre Hadids Enthusiasmus im Hinblick auf die Entwicklung der Kulturbauten gerechtfertigt, wenn sie feststellt: »Die Pläne, die von der Regierung Abu Dhabis für Saadiyat und den Kulturdistrikt konzipiert und entwickelt wurden, sind, kurz gesagt, außerordentlich. Wenn diese umfassende Vision Wirklichkeit wird, wird sie Standards für die globale Kultur setzen, die noch in Jahrzehnten Gültigkeit haben werden.«

Ce bâtiment de 62 m de haut devrait accueillir une salle de spectacles musicaux, une salle de concerts, un opéra, un théâtre et une salle polyvalente qui totaliseront 6300 places. Il constitue l'une des cinq institutions culturelles créées par la Compagnie d'investissement et de développement du tourisme d'Abu Dhabi (TDIC) avec l'assistance de la Salomon R. Guggenheim Foundation. En 2004, l'Autorité du Tourisme d'Abu Dhabi (ADTA) a confié à Gensler le plan directeur pour l'île de Saadiyat (Île du Bonheur), pour faire de ses 27 km² une « destination touristique de classe internationale respectueuse de l'environnement ». Le cœur de cette opération sera le quartier culturel de 270 hectares, planifié par Skidmore, Owings & Merrill (SOM), qui regroupera des réalisations de Tadao Ando, Jean Nouvel, Frank Gehry et Zaha Hadid. Celle-ci présente son projet de centre des arts du spectacle comme « une forme sculpturale qui émerge de l'intersection linéaire de cheminements piétonniers du quartier culturel et se développe peu à peu en un organisme qui projette un réseau de branches successives. En serpentant à travers le site, l'architecture croît en complexité, s'élaborant en hauteur et en profondeur, et poussant de multiples excroissances dans les parties abritant les lieux de spectacles, qui jaillissent de la structure comme les fruits d'une vigne ou regardent vers l'Ouest, vers la mer ». Zaha Hadid semble à juste titre enthousiaste sur le développement de ces nouveaux projets culturels puisqu'elle déclare par ailleurs : « Les plans pour l'île de Saadiyat et le quartier culturel, envisagés et développés par le gouvernement d'Abu Dhabi, sont tout simplement extraordinaires. Cette vision réalisée établira de nouveaux standards pour la culture globale qui exerceront leur influence pendant les décennies à venir. »

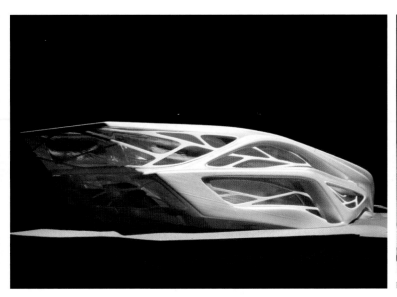
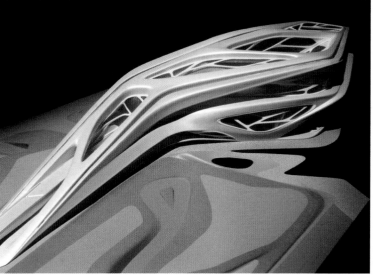

As is the case in a number of Zaha Hadid's recent projects, the lines of this design appear to emerge from the earth and to run forward (into the sea in this instance), almost like a living creature.

Wie bei einigen neueren Projekten Zaha Hadids scheinen die Linien dieses Entwurfs aus der Erde aufzutauchen und nach vorne zu fließen (in diesem Fall Richtung Meer) – ähnlich wie bei einem lebendigen Wesen.

Comme dans la plupart des projets récents de Zaha Hadid, les lignes d'ensemble semblent s'extraire de la terre pour se jeter au loin (ici dans la mer), presque comme une créature vivante.

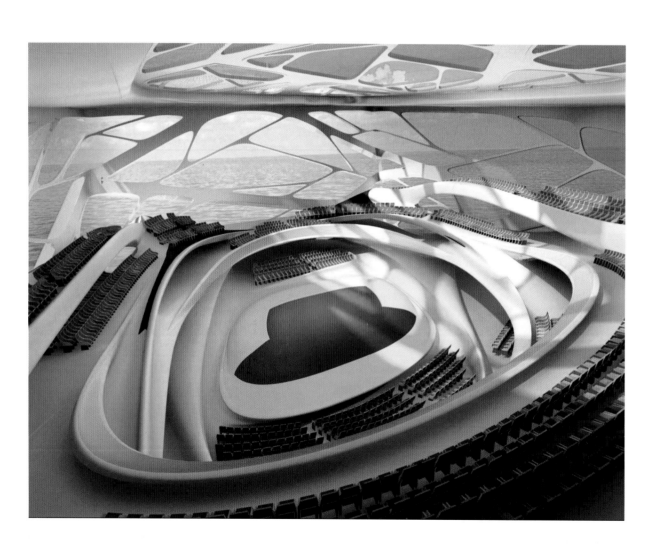

A spectacular perspective of an auditorium design for the complex shows how interior design corresponds to the architecture and is resolved in an efficient manner.

Die spektakuläre Perspektive eines Auditoriums für den Komplex zeigt die Kongruenz von Innen- und Außenarchitektur sowie die Effizienz der Raumgestaltung.

Perspective spectaculaire d'un projet d'auditorium pour le complexe, montrant comment l'architecture intérieure s'intègre avec efficacité aux plans d'ensemble.

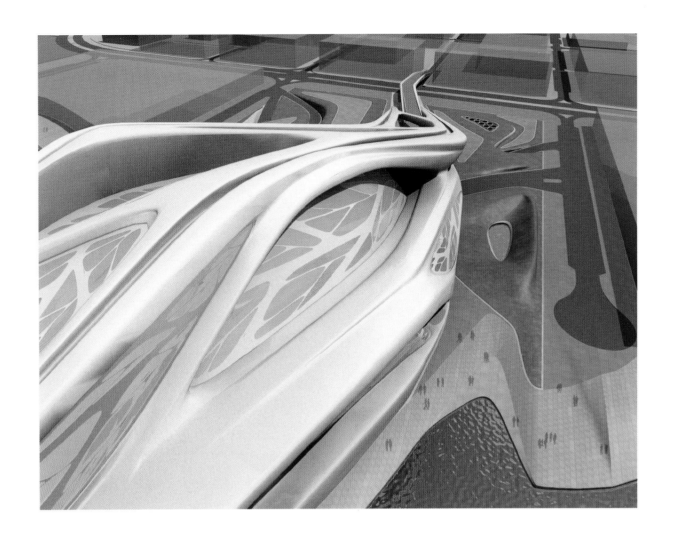

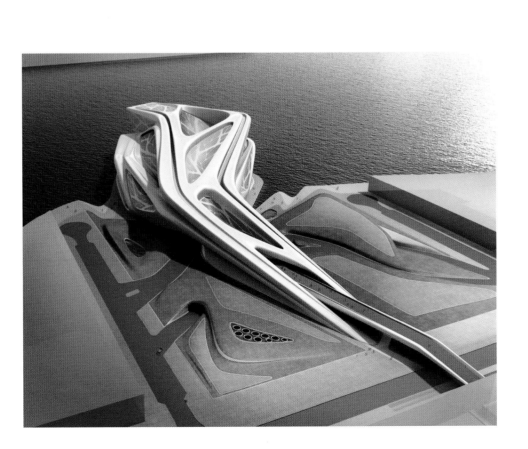

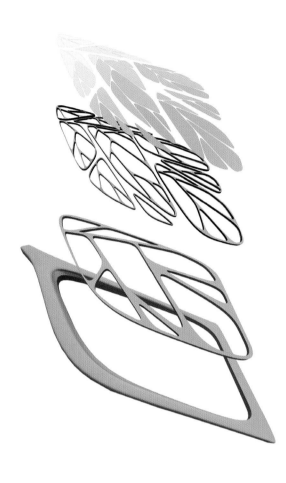

Hadid has managed the transition from architecture that exists only in the form of drawings or paintings to the "reality" of construction with surprising ease. Straight lines have been banished in the leaf-like designs seen here.

Hadid ist der Wechsel von Architektur, die nur als Zeichnung oder Bild existiert, in die »Realität« des Bauens überraschend leicht gelungen. Gerade Linien wurden aus den hier gezeigten blattähnlichen Formen völlig verbannt.

Hadid réussit avec une facilité surprenante la transition de l'architecture picturale à la réalité d'une construction. Les lignes droites ont disparu au profit de motifs en feuilles que l'on voit ici.

OPUS OFFICE TOWER
DUBAI, UAE
2007-10

FLOOR AREA: 85 641 m^2
CLIENT: Omniyat Properties COST: £ 235 million
CLIENT REPRESENTATIVE: Graham Hallett
PROJECT ARCHITECT: Christos Passas
TEAM MANAGER: Vincent Nowak
PROJECT TEAM: Chiara Ferrari, Wenyuan Peng,
Paul Peyrer-Heimstaett, Javier Ernesto Lebie,
Phivos Skroumbelos, Marilena Sophocleous
LOCAL ARCHITECT: Arex Consultants

Located in the Business Bay development area of Dubai, this new mixed-use commercial and retail complex will be set close to the area of the Burj Dubai tower and Hadid's own Signature Towers (see page 86). It is also close to the Dubai International Finance Center (see page 68). The visible form is that of a large cube that appears to "hover off the ground," although the design in fact consists of three separate towers 93 meters high. A freely formed void cuts into these volumes, while the ground floor "is developed as a transparent open field with multiple pathways that are drawn into the interior of the plan areas within the two separate lobbies." The void is lit from within at night, in a sense reversing the volumetric appearance of the building. Pixelated striations are to be applied to the glass façade reducing solar gain and giving it "a degree of reflectivity and materiality." The architects explain that "it is clear that from its inception this concept seeks interconnectedness and uniqueness. By applying these two qualities to our design repertoire, our research allowed us to provide unique, variable and fluid spaces within the project." Zaha Hadid concludes, "This is a building that challenges traditional concepts of office space. Not only will it be visually stunning, it will also be a workable space, and a place that allows every occupant to experience a better quality working environment, using the very latest technological advances."

Der gemischt genutzte Komplex mit Büro- und Verkaufsflächen in Dubais Stadtentwicklungsgebiet Business Bay wird sich in der Nähe des Burj Dubai sowie Hadids Signature Towers (Seite 86) befinden. Auch das Dubai International Financial Center (Seite 68) ist nicht weit entfernt. Die Grundform ist die eines großen Würfels, der scheinbar »über dem Erdboden schwebt«. Tatsächlich besteht der Komplex jedoch aus drei einzelnen 93 m hohen Türmen. Der frei geformte Raum zwischen den Baukörpern schneidet in die Türme ein. Das Erdgeschoss ist »als transparentes offenes Feld entworfen, mit vielen Durchwegungen, die in die Grundrisse bzw. in die voneinander unabhängigen Lobbys hineingeschrieben sind«. Nachts wird der Raum zwischen den Baukörpern von innen beleuchtet; dann scheint sich das volumetrische Erscheinungsbild des Baukörpers umzukehren. Auf die Glasfassaden sollen Pixelstreifen aufgebracht werden, die die Aufheizung des Gebäudes reduzieren und für »ein bestimmtes Maß an Reflexion und Materialität sorgen«. Die Architektin erläutert: »Von Anfang an lautete das Thema dieses Projekts Vernetzung und Einzigartigkeit. Indem wir diese Qualitäten in den Entwurf einfließen ließen, konnten wir unverwechselbare, flexible und fließende Räume realisieren.« Sie schließt mit der Aussage: »Dieses Projekt fordert traditionelle Vorstellungen von Büroräumen heraus. Es wird nicht nur optisch beeindrucken, es wird auch funktionieren und ein Ort sein, der allen Nutzern durch die Bereitstellung der neuesten technologischen Möglichkeiten ein hochwertiges Arbeitsumfeld bietet.«

Situé dans la zone de développement de la Business Bay à Dubaï, ce nouveau complexe de bureaux et de commerces voisinera avec la Burj Dubai et les Signature Towers de Hadid (voir page 86). Il est également proche du Dubai International Finance Center (voir page 68). Sa forme fait penser à un gigantesque cube « flottant au-dessus du sol », bien qu'il se compose en fait de trois tours séparées de 93 mètres de haut. Un vide de forme organique découpe ce cube en ces trois volumes, tandis que le rez-de-chaussée « est traité en espace ouvert transparent, sillonné de multiples cheminements qui se poursuivent dans les deux grands halls d'accueil indépendants ». La nuit, ce vide est éclairé de l'intérieur ce qui, en un sens, inverse la volumétrie de l'ensemble. Des stries pixellisées appliquées sur la façade réduisent le gain solaire et lui assurent « un certain de degré de réflexion et de matérialité ». Les architectes expliquent « qu'il est clair depuis le départ que ce concept est à la recherche à la fois d'interconnexion et d'unicité. En appliquant ces deux qualités à notre outillage conceptuel, nous avons pu créer des espaces uniques, variables et fluides à l'intérieur du projet. » Zaha Hadid conclut : « C'est un immeuble qui remet en cause les concepts traditionnels de l'espace de bureaux. Non seulement il sera visuellement étonnant, mais offrira aussi un espace favorable au travail, et un lieu qui permettra à chaque occupant de découvrir une meilleure qualité d'environnement de travail où il utilisera les dernières avancées technologiques. »

The continuity of the interior design with exterior forms is expressed here in a relatively restrained manner, and yet the whole flows from the exterior to the interior in an effortless continuum.

Die Kontinuität zwischen innen und außen findet bei diesem Projekt einen relativ zurückhaltenden Ausdruck, und doch geht die äußere Gestaltung mühelos in die der Innenräume über.

La continuité entre l'architecture intérieure et les formes extérieures s'exprime de façon relativement retenue, mais dans une dynamique qui va du dehors vers le dedans dans un continuum sans effort.

Night lighting of the building and the contrast between its freely formed void and the actual buildings define the appearance of the Opus Tower and assure that it looks like nothing else being planned in Dubai.

Die nächtliche Beleuchtung und der Kontrast zwischen dem frei geformten Zwischenraum und den Gebäuden bestimmen die äußere Erscheinung des Opus Towers und sorgen dafür, dass dieses Projekt mit keiner anderen Planung für Dubai zu vergleichen ist.

L'éclairage nocturne de l'immeuble et le contraste entre son énorme vide de forme libre et les immeubles avoisinants définit l'aspect d'Opus Tower qui ne ressemblent à rien d'autre d'existant ou de prévu à Dubaï.

SIGNATURE TOWERS BUSINESS BAY
DUBAI, UAE 2006 -

AREA: 500 000 m²
CLIENT: Dubai Properties COST: not disclosed
DESIGN: Zaha Hadid with Patrik Schumacher
PROJECT ARCHITECT: Chris Lepine
PROJECT DIRECTOR: Lars Teichmann
PROJECT TEAM: Chris Lepine, Stephan Wurster, Eren Ciraci, Alessio Constantini, David Campos, Hoda Nobakhti, Chryssanthi Perpatidou, Bowornwan May Noradee, Nahed Jawad, Hussam Chakouf, Bassam Al Shiekh, Daniel Norell, Tomas Rabl, Chiara Ferrari, Erhan Patat
PROJECT ARCHITECT (COMPETITION): Tiago Correia
DESIGN TEAM (COMPETITION): Ana Cajiao, Saleem Abdel-Jalil, Sophie Le Bienvenu, Hooman Talebi, Mathias Reisigl, Diego Rosales, Tyen Masten, Daewha Kang, Renos Constantino, Graham Modlen

Set to be a central element of the rapidly developing Business Bay area being created not far from the Burj Dubai Tower by Dubai Properties, the Signature Towers are designed for mixed use, including offices, hotel, residential, and retail space. The complex includes two link bridges, waterfront park, and promenade. The triple tower design is extremely unusual insofar as its fluid lines are concerned. The architects write, "The three towers rise above the creek and project themselves as an icon for the surrounding developments and for the Gulf region. The towers' striking design creates a new presence that punctures the skyline with a powerful recognizable silhouette. The fluid character of the towers is generated through an intrinsically dynamic composition of volumes. The towers are intertwined to share programmatic elements and rotate to maximize the views from the site toward the creek and neighboring developments." Although work in the area was not very far advanced in mid-2007, plans call for direct connections to main thoroughfares such as Sheikh Zayed Road. The site is composed of four different elements, leading to the idea of a "woven" combination of connections and linking public spaces, and the tripartite tower configuration was developed as a result of the requirement to provide hotel, residential, and office space. A shared base or podium underlines the connectivity of the towers and suggests a continual movement of activities and users within the complex. Large multiuse complexes such as this one are numerous in the planned architecture of Dubai, but they often tend to create an image of disconnection or disembodiment, while Hadid has on the contrary sought an inviting movement, sure to remain "iconic" no matter what odd shapes may be looming on the horizon, but also deliberately and effectively connected to the emerging city.

Als zentraler Baustein der sich rasant entwickelnden Business Bay sollen die Signature Towers in der Nähe des Burj Dubai verschiedene Nutzungen enthalten, darunter Büros, ein Hotel, Wohnungen und Läden. Bauherr ist Dubai Properties. Zwei Verbindungsbrücken, ein Uferpark und eine Promenade gehören ebenfalls zu dem Komplex. Kennzeichnend für die Gebäudegruppe sind die fließenden Linien der drei Türme. Die Architekten schreiben: »Die sich über den Fluss erhebenden Türme könnten als Logo für die Bauvorhaben in der Umgebung und in der Region fungieren. Die ungewöhnliche Gestaltung verleiht ihnen eine neuartige Präsenz, die die Skyline um eine kraftvolle, wiedererkennbare Silhouette bereichert. Die fließende Gestalt der Baukörper ergibt sich aus der dynamischen Komposition der Volumen. Um eine gemeinsame Nutzung bestimmter Funktionsbereiche zu ermöglichen, sind die Türme miteinander verbunden. Um Ausblicke auf den Fluss und benachbarte Gebäude zu gewähren, drehen sie sich um ihre eigene Achse.« Mitte 2007 waren die Arbeiten noch nicht sehr weit fortgeschritten, ge-

plant sind jedoch direkte Verbindungen zu den Hauptverkehrswegen, z. B. der Scheich-Zayed-Straße. Der aus insgesamt vier verschiedenen Elementen bestehende Entwurf erweckt den Eindruck einer »gewebten« Verknüpfung von Verbindungen und vernetzten öffentlichen Räumen. Die dreiteilige Turmkonfiguration wurde aus den geforderten Nutzungen – einem Hotel, Wohnungen sowie Büros – entwickelt. Ein gemeinsamer Unterbau unterstreicht die Einheit der Türme und fördert eine ständige Bewegung der Aktivitäten und Nutzer innerhalb der Gebäudegruppe. Große gemischt genutzte Bauvorhaben wie dieses gibt es in Dubai viele. Oft wirken sie jedoch sehr auf sich selbst bezogen und entmaterialisiert. Hadid dagegen hat versucht, eine einladende Geste zu schaffen. Ganz gleich was für merkwürdige Formen noch am Horizont auftauchen werden – dieses Projekt wird seine Zeichenhaftigkeit bewahren und gleichzeitig bewusst und effektiv mit dem entstehenden Stadtteil verbunden sein.

Principaux composants de la zone de Business Bay en plein développement et non loin de la Burj Dubai des Dubai Properties, les Signature Towers sont conçues pour un usage mixte : bureaux, hôtel, appartements et commerces. Ce complexe de trois tours extrêmement surprenantes par leur fluidité couvre également deux ponts, un parc en front de mer et une promenade. Selon les architectes : « Les trois tours s'élèvent au-dessus de la crique et se projettent volontairement en icônes du développement de leur environnement et de la région du Golfe. Leur dessin étonnant crée une présence nouvelle qui marque le panorama de sa puissante silhouette, aisément reconnaissable. Le caractère fluide vient d'une composition de volumes intrinsèquement dynamique. Elles sont imbriquées pour partager leurs composants programmatiques et pivotent pour optimiser les vues vers la crique et l'urbanisation environnante. » L'ensemble prévoit une liaison directe avec de grands axes de circulation comme la voie Cheikh Zayed. Le site se compose de quatre éléments différents d'où l'idée de combinaison « tissée » de connexions et de liens avec les espaces publics. La configuration tripartite vient de la triple fonction attendue : hôtel, appartements et bureaux. Un podium commun regroupe les interconnexions des tours et anticipe un échange continu d'activités entre les usagers du complexe. Les grands ensembles polyvalents de ce type sont nombreux dans les plans de développement de Dubaï, mais tendent souvent à donner une image de déconnexion et de démembrement, alors qu'Hadid, au contraire, a cherché à créer un mouvement fédérateur, certaine que ces tours resteront « iconiques » quelles que soient les formes bizarres qui se profilent à l'horizon mais aussi efficacement connectées à une cité en pleine émergence.

The dancing, swaying movement of the towers, rising from their shared podium, appears to challenge the principles of engineering, placing the bulk of the apparent weight of at least one of the towers in perilous equilibrium.

Die tanzende, schwingende Bewegung der sich auf einem gemeinsamen Podest erhebenden Türme scheint die Gesetze der Statik herauszufordern, indem sie den Hauptteil der Last zumindest eines der Türme in gefährliches Ungleichgewicht verschiebt.

Le mouvement de danse et de déhanchement des tours dressées sur un même podium semble remettre en cause certains principes physiques, en allant, par exemple, jusqu'à mettre la masse du poids apparent de l'une des tours en équilibre périlleux.

9

HOK SPORT

HOK SPORT
300 Wyandotte
Kansas City, Missouri 64105
United States

Tel: +1 816 221 1500
Fax: +1 816 221 1578
e-mail: sport@hoksve.com
Web: www.hoksport.com

HOK SPORT was created in 1983 when six architects working under the umbrella of the large St. Louis firm Hellmuth, Obata + Kassabaum (HOK) invented the first practice dedicated exclusively to the design of sport facilities. Through a merger with a similar company, LOBB Sport, with offices in London and Brisbane, Australia, and a home office in Kansas City, Missouri, HOK Sport became a global player sports design firm. In 2002, HOK Sport merged with Anderson Consulting Team, which specialized in public event planning. The activities of HOK Sport Avenue Event has a staff of more than 400 persons in offices in Kansas City, Nashville, Denver, London and Brisbane. The firm has had a role in more than 825 projects worth $20 billion. A designer of the Dubai Autodrome published here is John Barrow, a Principal of HOK Sport's London office. Barrow gained his Diploma in Architecture in his native Australia. His career led him to the United Kingdom where he built up a strong portfolio of sport and leisure projects and partnered with HOK Sport on the design of Sheffield Arena in 1990. His recent projects include the Faro and Benfica stadia completed for the Euro 2004 soccer championship in Portugal, and the Oval Lingotto for the 2006 Winter Olympics in Turin, Italy.

DUBAI AUTODROME
DUBAI, UAE
2000 - 04

ARCHITECT PARTNER: HOK Dubai
TOTAL SITE AREA: 2.8 million m² CIRCUIT FOOTPRINT: 929 000 m²
CLIENT: Union Properties PJSC COST: $4.9 million
STRUCTURAL ENGINEER: Buro Happold PROJECT MANAGEMENT: Edara
PROJECT TEAM: John Barrow, Ivar Krasinski,
Partho Dutta, Martin Baerschmidt
LANDSCAPE ARCHITECT: HOK/Al Khatib Cracknell
TRACK DESIGNERS: West Surrey Racing

The client imagined a "futuristic" complex including racing, recreation, retail, and residential space. The first structure completed was the marketing and management building, followed by the racetrack and grandstand. Located at the highest point on a desert site 25 minutes by car from central Dubai, the first building uses double-glazed low-e glass, and contains a viewing gallery as well as offices and conference rooms. Large aluminum cantilevers and the orientation of the building provide some relief from the intense afternoon sun. As the architects explain, "The architectural style of this complex and its signature marketing and management building draw from concepts central to motor sports and racing. Chief among these is the idea of dynamic balance—that fine line between speed and traction, between motion and control. Dynamic balance is achieved on the track when a driver balances the centrifugal force of corners and pushes the limits of possibility. The marketing and management building captures that feeling with a structure that appears active, figuratively 'leaning into the turns.' The dynamic balance established in the marketing and management building's design is echoed in other buildings throughout the complex. This creates a continuity of form from building to building, and makes the development instantly recognizable." The first fully integrated motor sports facility in the region, the complex includes a 5.39-kilometer circuit, with six possible configurations, a race and driving school and a carting track, but it can also be used for concerts or corporate events. The facility's largest structure is the 7000-seat grandstand in phase I, expandable to 15 000, all with direct views of the Burj Al Arab hotel (see page 42).

Der Bauherr stellte sich eine futuristische Anlage mit einer Rennstrecke, Freizeiteinrichtungen, Verkaufsflächen und einem Wohnbereich vor. Das Marketing- und Managementgebäude wurde zuerst fertiggestellt, es folgten die Rennstrecke und die Haupttribüne. Der gesamte Komplex liegt in der Wüste und ist in 25 Minuten mit dem Auto von Dubais Zentrum zu erreichen. Das Marketing- und Managementgebäude befindet sich auf dem höchsten Punkt des Geländes und ist mit einer zweischaligen Konstruktion aus Low-e-Glas (Wärmedämmglas) ausgestattet. Es umfasst eine Tribüne, Büros und Konferenzräume. Große Vordächer aus Aluminium und die Orientierung des Gebäudes ergänzen den Schutz vor der intensiven Nachmittagssonne. Die Architekten erläutern: »Das architektonische Konzept des gesamten Komplexes und des markanten Marketing- und Managementgebäudes ist dem Motor- und Rennsport entlehnt. Im Mittelpunkt steht dabei die Idee einer dynamischen Balance – die Balance zwischen Geschwindigkeit und Zugkraft, zwischen Bewegung und Kontrolle. Eine dynamische Balance auf der Rennstrecke wird erreicht, wenn der Fahrer die Zentrifugalkräfte in den Kurven

ausgleicht und die Grenzen des Möglichen erweitert. Das Gebäude fängt dieses Gefühl ein, indem es als aktives Element wirkt und so aussieht, ›als würde es sich in die Kurve legen‹. Die dynamische Balance, die das Gebäude thematisiert, findet in den anderen Gebäuden auf dem Gelände seinen Widerhall. Dadurch wird eine formale Einheitlichkeit der Bauten geschaffen, die für einen hohen Wiedererkennungswert des Komplexes sorgt.« Die erste für verschiedene Rennen nutzbare Motorsporteinrichtung in der Region umfasst eine 5,39 km lange Strecke mit sechs möglichen Konfigurationen, eine Renn- und Fahrschule und eine Kartstrecke, sie kann aber auch für Konzerte oder für Unternehmensveranstaltungen genutzt werden. Das größte Gebäude des ersten Bauabschnitts ist die Haupttribüne mit 7000 Plätzen, die später auf 15 000 Plätze erweitert werden kann und einen unverbauten Ausblick auf das Hotel Burj al-Arab bietet (S. 42).

Ce complexe « futuriste », comprenant des circuits de course, des installations de loisirs, des commerces et des logements, a été imaginé par le client. La première construction achevée a été l'immeuble regroupant les services de gestion et de commercialisation, suivi par les pistes et une grande tribune. Implanté sur le point le plus élevé d'un terrain situé dans le désert à 25 minutes de voiture du centre de Dubaï, ce premier immeuble est habillé d'un double vitrage à basse énergie. Il contient une galerie-observatoire, des bureaux et des salles de conférences. De grands auvents d'aluminium en porte-à-faux et l'orientation générale du bâtiment protègent en partie de l'intensité du soleil de l'après-midi. Comme l'expliquent les architectes : « Le style architectural de ce complexe et de son bâtiment administratif qui sera son symbole visuel est issu de concepts tirés des sports et courses automobiles. L'idée principale est celle d'équilibre dynamique, cette mince limite entre vitesse et traction, mouvement et contrôle. L'équilibre dynamique est atteint sur piste lorsque le pilote équilibre la force centrifuge dans un virage et pousse les possibilités de la voiture dans ses limites. Ce bâtiment a capté cette impression et paraît actif, figurativement « penché dans les virages ». Son équilibre dynamique se retrouve en écho dans d'autres réalisations du complexe, afin de créer une continuité de formes d'un bâtiment à l'autre et donner à l'ensemble une personnalité immédiatement identifiable. » Premier complexe de sport automobile entièrement intégré construit dans la région, l'ensemble comprend un circuit de 5,39 km à six configurations possibles, une école de conduite et de compétition, une piste de karting et peut également servir pour des concerts ou des événements d'entreprise. La plus importante construction est la tribune de 7000 places (phase 1), d'où l'on aperçoit l'hôtel Burj Al Arab (voir page 42). Elle pourra s'agrandir jusqu'à 15 000 places.

The raking cantilevered forms of the buildings are certainly well chosen in the context of automobile racing. Above all, the complex gives an impression not only of movement but of exciting design.

Im Kontext des Motorsports sind die auskragenden, sich nach vorne lehnenden Gebäude sicher eine gute Wahl. Die Anlage vermittelt dadurch nicht nur den Eindruck von Bewegung, sondern bietet auch eine spannende Gestaltung.

Les formes inclinées et en porte-à-faux des bâtiments sont certainement un bon choix dans le contexte d'un circuit de compétition automobile. Le complexe donne par-dessus tout une impression de mouvement et un design excitant.

The cantilevered marketing and management building (above) is designed with a racecar engine in mind. Below, the dramatically cantilevered viewing stands.

Beim Entwurf des sich nach vorne lehnenden Marketing and Management Building (oben) stand der Motor eines Rennautos Pate; unten die dramatisch auskragende Tribüne.

L'immeuble en porte-à-faux du marketing et de la gestion (ci-dessus) a été conçu en pensant à une voiture de course. Ci-dessous, les tribunes au porte-à-faux spectaculaire.

10

KAZUHIRO KOJIMA + KAZUKO AKAMATSU/C + A

CAt (C + A TOKYO)
4F Kyuseigun Building
1-20-5, Ebisu-nishi
Shibuya-ku, Tokyo, 150–0021,
Japan

Tel: +81 3 5489 8264
Fax: +81 3 5458 6117
e-mail: info@c-and-a.co.jp
Web: www.c-and-a.co.jp

KAZUHIRO KOJIMA was born in Osaka in Japan in 1958. He received his B.Arch degree from Kyoto University (1982) and his M.Arch from the University of Tokyo (1984). In 1986, he established Coelacanth Architects Inc. with a staff of seven in Tokyo. He is a Professor at the Science University of Tokyo and a Visiting Professor at the Kyoto Institute of Technology. In 2005, he reorganized his firm as C+A Coelacanth and Associates, and is the CEO of that firm. His associate Kazuko Akamatsu was born in 1968 in Tokyo and received her B.Arch from the Japan Women's University in 1990. She became a partner in C+A in 2000. Their firm was reorganized in 2005 as CAt (C+A Tokyo) and CAn (C+A Nagoya). Their built work includes the Utase Elementary School, Chiba, Japan (1995); Hakuou High School, Sendai, Japan (2001); Beijing Jian Wai SOHO / SOHO villa, Beijing, China (in collaboration with Riken Yamamoto, 2003); and the Liberal Arts and Science College, Doha, Qatar (with Arata Isozaki, 2004, published here). Ongoing projects include the Ho Chi Minh University of Architecture (a 102 000 m^2 complex in Ho Chi Minh City, Vietnam, 2006–) and a master plan and housing for Tianjin, China (2003–).

LIBERAL ARTS & SCIENCE COLLEGE
DOHA, QATAR
2001 · 05

AREA: 36 363 m²
CLIENT: Qatar Foundation for Science and Community Development
COST: not disclosed
STAFF ARCHITECTS: Kensuke Watanabe, Tomoya Oshika
MASTER PLAN, COORDINATION: Arata Isozaki and i-NET
PROJECT DIRECTOR: Shuichi Fujie, i-NET
PROJECT MANAGER: Shunji Nagata, i-NET

This two-story reinforced-concrete structure was part of a 408 000-square-meter master planning area developed by Arata Isozaki in the suburbs of Doha. "Here we have noted one of the features of Muslim culture, that their cities are assemblies of 'centers.' Unlike a city of another culture with a solid, symbolic center, a Muslim city encompasses numerous 'centers' each of which holds different activities. Inspired by those cities, we designed the building to contain many small patios." Thus, the exterior Winter Patios are comfortable in the winter, though too hot for use in the summer, and the Summer Patios housing the Flexible Learning Areas (FLA) are in air-conditioned atria. The architects also used the strong sunlight of Doha as a source of ideas. Double-roofed and double-skinned, the building is designed to provide year-round comfort. A system inspired by Middle Eastern wind towers is used to cool the air. Glass-fiber gypsum reflectors bring daylight even into spaces where direct exposure to sunlight would not be advisable. Successive louvers and iron shades give the impression that "walking around the building in the overlapping shadows, one might feel that he/she is enchanted by limitless veils." Only a minimum view to the outside is assured through small windows in order to preserve the environmental comfort of the interiors. Glass-fiber reinforced-concrete (GRC) panels are used on the exterior walls. Colored yellow on the underside and spaced 50 millimeters apart, these panels give a yellow glow to the inner walls. The overall plan of the building provides for one in every four façade surfaces to receive sunlight at any given time. Classrooms and the FLA areas are on the ground floor, while teachers' offices and "open resource areas" are located on the upper level. Circular lecture rooms connect the ground and upper levels.

Das zweigeschossige Stahlbetongebäude befindet sich auf einem 408 000 m² großen Areal am Stadtrand von Doha, für das Arata Isozaki einen Masterplan erstellte. Kazuhiro Kojima erläutert: »Kennzeichnend für die muslimische Kultur ist, dass die Städte aus einer Ansammlung von Zentren bestehen ... Davon ließen wir uns inspirieren und entwarfen ein Gebäude mit vielen kleinen Innenhöfen.« Die »Winterhöfe« sind im Winter angenehme Aufenthaltsbereiche, im Sommer ist es dort jedoch zu heiß. Die »Sommerhöfe« mit einem Zentrum für flexibles Lernen sind als klimatisierte Atrien gestaltet. Auch die intensive Sonneneinstrahlung inspirierte die Architekten. Das Gebäude ist sowohl mit einer doppelten Dachkonstruktion als auch mit einer Doppelfassade ausgestattet und bietet dadurch das ganze Jahr über ein angenehmes Raumklima. Die Kühlung der Luft erfolgt über ein System, das ähnlich wie die traditionellen Windtürme des Nahen Ostens funktioniert. Wo direktes Tageslicht nicht erwünscht ist, wird es indirekt über Reflektoren aus Glasfasergipskarton in die Räume gelenkt. Um das Klima im Inneren des Gebäudes zu schützen, sind die Fenster klein. Die Fassaden bestehen aus glasfaserverstärkten Betonpaneelen. Die Fugenbreite zwischen den innenseitig gelben Paneelen beträgt 50 mm. Dadurch entsteht auf der inneren Wandschale ein gelbes Muster. Aufgrund seiner Ausrichtung ist jeweils eine der vier Seiten des Gebäudes besonnt. Unterrichtsräume und das Zentrum für flexibles Lernen sind im Erdgeschoss angeordnet. Die Räume des Lehrpersonals sowie »offene Reserveräume« befinden sich im Obergeschoss. Kreisförmige Hörsäle verbinden beide Geschosse miteinander.

Cet immeuble de deux niveaux fait partie d'une zone de 408 000 m² dans la banlieue de Doha qui a été urbanisée par Arta Isozaki. « Nous avons remarqué que à la différence des cités d'autres cultures possédant un centre symbolique fort, la ville musulmane comprend plusieurs « centres », chacun exerçant des activités différentes. Inspirés par cette solution urbanistique, nous avons conçu cet immeuble doté de multiples petits patios. » Les patios « d'hiver » extérieurs sont confortables en hiver, mais trop chauds pour l'été, et les patios « d'été », qui abritent les zones « d'enseignement souple », bénéficient de la climatisation. Doté d'une double toiture et d'une double peau, le bâtiment est conçu pour assurer un confort permanent tout au long de l'année, quelle que soit l'intensité du soleil. Un système inspiré des tours à vent moyen-orientales sert à rafraîchir l'air. Des réflecteurs en plâtre armé de fibre de verre orientent la lumière naturelle vers des volumes où il n'est pas judicieux de la laisser pénétrer directement. Les petites fenêtres ne permettent que des perspectives limitées sur l'extérieur, afin de préserver le confort environnemental à l'intérieur. Sur les murs extérieurs, des panneaux en béton renforcé de fibre de verre à sous-face jaune, espacés de 50 m, créent un motif de même couleur sur les murs intérieurs. Le plan d'ensemble de l'immeuble fait qu'une façade sur quatre seulement est exposée à la fois et à certains moments au soleil direct. Les salles de cours sont au rez-de-chaussée, les bureaux et les zones de « ressources en libre accès » au niveau supérieur. Des salles de lecture, circulaires, font lien entre le rez-de-chaussée et les niveaux supérieurs.

Within a rectangular plan, the architects introduce substantial variety through the irregular openings in the façades and the circular lecture halls visible in the plan below.

Mit den unregelmäßigen Fassadenöffnungen und den kreisrunden Hörsälen (zu sehen im Grundriss unten) bieten die Architekten in dem rechteckigen Baukörper eine große Vielfalt an.

Dans le cadre d'un plan au sol strictement orthogonal, les architectes ont introduit une subtile diversité par des ouvertures irrégulières pratiquées dans les façades et par des salles de lecture circulaires visibles dans le plan ci-dessous.

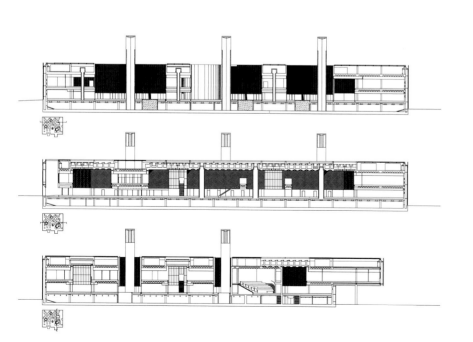
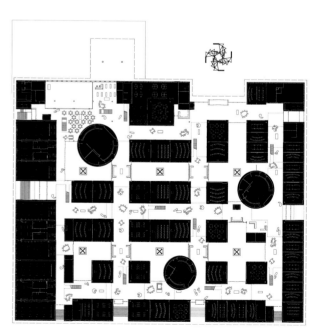

Variety is introduced in an otherwise relatively practical building by such features as the ceiling design intended to bring in natural light seen above.

Oben: Gestaltungselemente wie die Decke beleben das ansonsten eher strenge und funktionale Gebäude und begünstigen den Einfall von natürlichem Licht.

L'animation est introduite dans ce bâtiment par ailleurs relativement fonctionnel par des éléments inattendus comme le dessin du plafond ci-dessus conçu pour apporter la lumière du jour.

11

KPF

**KOHN PEDERSEN FOX ASSOCIATES
(INTERNATIONAL) PA**
13 Langley Street
London WC2H 9JG
United Kingdom

Tel: +44 20 78 36 66 68
Fax: +44 20 74 97 11 75
Web: www.kpf.com

KPF was founded in 1976. With offices in New York, London and Shanghai, KPF currently has work in 30 countries. KPF's projects of note include the DG Bank Headquarters, Frankfurt, Germany (1993); the World Bank, Washington, D. C. (1996); IBM Corporate Headquarters, Armonk, New York (1997); and the Shanghai World Financial Center, Shanghai (2004–08), currently the tallest building in China. David Leventhal, a member of the firm since 1979, helped to found the London studio with Lee Polisano in 1989. As Principal in charge of design, Leventhal collaborated on the design of the Abu Dhabi Investment Authority (ADIA) Headquarters with Senior Associate Principal and Senior Designer, Kevin Flanagan. ADIA incorporates low-energy design strategies for hot, dry climates, a feature representative of KPF's approach to sustainable design. Leventhal and Flanagan's previous collaborations include the Chicago Title and Trust Building in Chicago, and De Hoftoren in The Hague, The Netherlands. Their designs are "a series of investigations into the nature of the workplace." De Hoftoren won first prize in the inaugural International High-Rise Competition, hosted by the Frankfurt Architectural Museum.

ADIA HEADQUARTERS
ABU DHABI, UAE
2001-07

AREA: 87 300 m^2; 29 600 m^2 (separate parking structure)
CLIENT: Abu Dhabi Investment Authority
COST: not disclosed
PROJECT DESIGNERS: Kevin Flanagan, David Leventhal

The architects based their design in part on the strong urban grid of the city of Abu Dhabi.

"The wing to the north follows the city grid while the wing to the south appears to open like a book, opening to the sea, the vista and toward Mecca," say the architects. "We thought of a space that would be like a courtyard, in the tradition of Islamic architecture. Here the courtyard is formed by two bars set apart as wings connected by a central vertical courtyard atrium. The opening draws the sea and green of the Corniche into the building. A series of gardens in the sky become an extension of the green parkway." The Abu Dhabi Investment Authority requested large central common zones on each floor, and KPF responded with a vertical atrium garden. The architects have given importance to the relationship of the site to the green zones of the city. As they say, "The key to the design is the acknowledgement of the profound importance of the sea in the development of the site and of the urban plan as a garden city." Extensive ground-floor planting "reinforces the original urban landscape strategy, tying our site to the urban plan." A 250-seat auditorium is part of the project near the entry level. Shaped like an undulating sheet of paper, the KPF double-tower design on the New Corniche Road brings an original tower to a city whose burgeoning development, like that of other urban areas in the region, is very much in need of quality architecture.

Ein bestimmender Faktor für den Entwurf war das strenge städtebauliche Raster von Abu Dhabi.

»Der nördliche Teil des Gebäudes folgt dem Straßenraster; der südliche Teil wirkt, als würde er sich wie ein Buch zum Meer, zur schönsten Aussicht und nach Mekka hin öffnen«, erläutern die Architekten. »Wir dachten an einen hofartigen Raum in der Tradition islamischer Architektur. Hier wird der Hof durch zwei flügelähnliche Riegel gebildet, die durch das Atrium miteinander verbunden sind. Die sich öffnende Form zieht das Meer und die Vegetation an der Corniche in das Gebäude hinein. Eine Abfolge von ›Himmelsgärten‹ erweitert die begrünte Uferstraße.« Die Abu Dhabi Investment Authority wünschte großzügige zentrale Gemeinschaftsbereiche in jedem Geschoss. KPF kam diesem Wunsch durch das begrünte, über alle Geschosse reichende Atrium nach. Die Architekten legen Wert auf die Verknüpfung des Grundstücks mit den Grünflächen der Stadt. Sie sagen: »Im Mittelpunkt des Entwurfs steht die Anerkennung der zentralen Bedeutung des Meers für die Bebauung des Grundstücks und für die städtebauliche Entwicklung von Doha als einer Gartenstadt.« Die intensive Bepflanzung des Grundstücks »verstärkt die übergeordnete Strategie einer Stadtlandschaft, die den Standort mit der städtebaulichen Ordnung verzahnt«. In der Nähe der Eingangsebene ist ein Veranstaltungssaal mit 250 Plätzen angeordnet. Der Doppelturm von KPF mit seiner an gewelltes Papier erinnernden Form ist ein formal eigenständiges Hochhaus an der New Corniche Road. Wie auch für andere Städte in der Region ist gute Architektur für Dohas aufkeimende Entwicklung von zentraler Bedeutung.

La conception du projet s'appuie sur la trame urbaine en grille de la ville d'Abu Dhabi.

« L'aile nord suit la trame tandis que l'aile sud semble s'ouvrir comme un livre sur la mer, la vue, et vers La Mecque », expliquent les architectes. « Nous avons pensé à un espace proche de la cour qui existe dans la tradition architecturale islamique. Ici, cette cour est délimitée par deux barres en aile connectées par un atrium central vertical. L'ouverture laisse pénétrer la mer et la nature verdoyante de la Corniche dans le bâtiment. La succession de jardins suspendus devient une extension de l'avenue plantée. » L'autorité d'investissement d'Abu Dhabi voulait pouvoir disposer de vastes zones centrales communes à chaque niveau, demande à laquelle les architectes ont répondu par un atrium-jardin vertical. La relation du site avec les zones vertes de la ville a été particulièrement prise en compte : « La clé de ce projet est la reconnaissance de l'importance profonde de la mer dans le développement de ce site et d'un plan d'urbanisme de ville-jardin. » D'abondantes plantations en rez-de-chaussée « renforcent la stratégie du paysagisme urbain d'origine, et lient notre intervention au plan directeur ». Un auditorium de 250 places est implanté près du niveau de l'entrée. Comme une feuille de papier ondulé, cette double tour sur la nouvelle route de la Corniche apporte une forme originale à une ville dont le développement rapide, comme celui d'autres centres urbains de la région, manque souvent d'architecture de qualité.

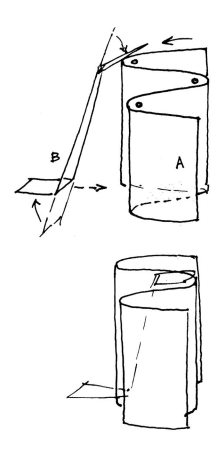

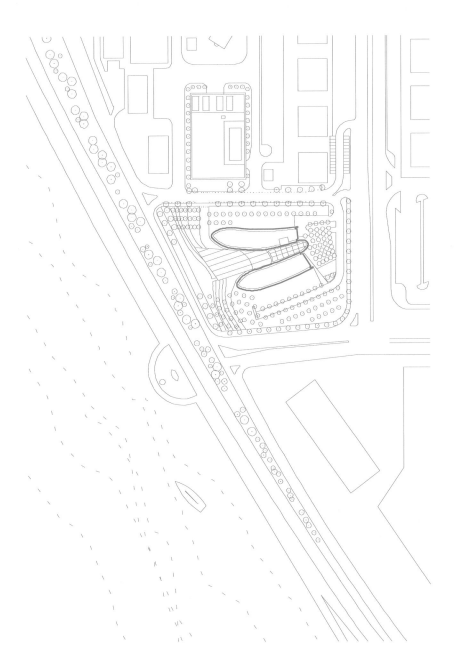

As the drawing above shows, the basic plan of the buildings is inspired by an undulating band. The curvature of the buildings and such features as the canopy-screen seen below give a dynamic feeling to the entire complex.

Wie die Skizze zeigt, beruht das Konzept des Gebäudes auf einem gewellten Band. Die Kurven und Elemente wie etwa das Vordach verleihen dem Gebäude Dynamik.

Comme le montre le dessin ci-dessus, le plan des immeubles est inspiré d'un bandeau sinueux. Les courbes des bâtiments et certains éléments caractéristiques comme l'auvent ci-dessous donnent un sentiment général de dynamisme.

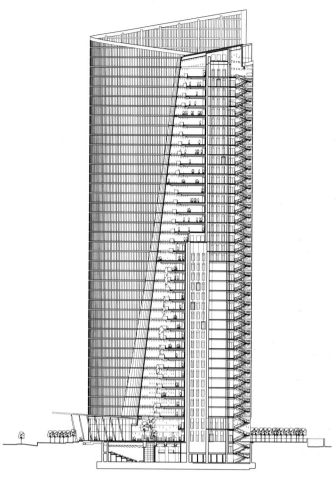

An atrium slices up through the building bringing daylight and a bit of drama into the core of the tower. The rounded angles of the leading edges of the building offer spectacular views of the area.

Das Atrium zerteilt das Gebäude, lässt Tageslicht ins Innere und verleiht ihm Dramatik. Die gerundeten Gebäudeenden bieten spektakuläre Ausblicke auf die Umgebung.

L'atrium se fraye son chemin à travers l'immeuble pour apporter la lumière naturelle et un peu d'animation jusqu'au cœur de la tour. Les angles arrondis des principales avancées des façades offrent des vues spectaculaires sur les environs.

12

JEAN NOUVEL

ATELIERS JEAN NOUVEL
10, Cité d'Angoulème
75011 Paris
France

Tel: +33 1 49 23 83 83
Fax: +33 1 43 14 81 10
e-mail: info@jeannouvel.fr
Web: www.jeannouvel.com

Born in 1945 in Fumel, France, **JEAN NOUVEL** studied in Bordeaux and then at the Paris École des Beaux-Arts (1964–72). From 1967 to 1970, he was an assistant of Claude Parent and Paul Virilio. In 1970, he created his first office with François Seigneur. His first widely noticed project was the Institut du Monde Arabe, Paris (with Architecture Studio, 1981–87). Other works include his Nemausus Housing, Nîmes (1985–87); Lyon Opera House, (1986–93); Vinci Conference Center, Tours (1989–93); Euralille Shopping Center, Lille (1991–94); Fondation Cartier, Paris (1991–94), all in France; and Galeries Lafayette, Berlin, Germany (1992–95). His unbuilt projects include the 400-meter-tall "Tours sans fins," La Défense, Paris (1989); Grand Stade for the 1998 World Cup, Paris (1994); and Tenaga National Tower, Kuala Lumpur, Malaysia (1995). In 2003, Jean Nouvel won a competition sponsored by the Aga Khan Trust for Culture for the design of the waterfront Corniche in Doha, Qatar, and was called on to design the new Guggenheim Museum in Rio de Janeiro, Brazil. His major completed projects since 2000 are the Music and Conference Center, Lucerne, Switzerland (1992–2000); the Agbar Tower, Barcelona, Spain (1999–2005); social housing at the Cité Manifeste, Mulhouse, France (2001–05); the extension of the Reina Sofia Museum, Madrid, Spain (1999–2005); the Quai Branly Museum, Paris, France (1999–2006); an apartment building in SoHo, New York (2003–07); and the Guthrie Theater, Minneapolis, Minnesota (2001–06). Current projects also include port facilities in Le Havre (planned for 2007) and the city hall in Montpellier (2002–09), both in France. Jean Nouvel received the RIBA Gold Medal in 2001.

DOHA HIGH RISE OFFICE BUILDING
DOHA, QATAR
2003-10

AREA: 110 000 m²
CLIENT: H.E. Sheikh Saud al-Thani
COST: €100 million
PREPARATORY STUDIES: Ingrid
Menon, Hafid Rakem

This 231-meter-high tower was designed in the midst of the extensive cultural development plans launched by Sheik Saud al-Thani, and is situated between the new city center and the Corniche on the north side of Doha Bay. Calling on ideas that Nouvel first developed in his unbuilt "Tour sans fins" (Paris, 1989), and more recently in the Agbar Tower (Barcelona, 2000–05), the new building relies on a circular plan with structural elements grouped on the periphery rather than in the core. The Doha building, round like its forebears, measures 45 meters in diameter and is topped by a dome. Butterfly aluminum elements "echoing the geometric complexity of the *mashrabiyya*" are set on the façade according to the specific orientation of each part of the building—25 % toward north, 40 % toward south, 60 % on east and west. Beneath this layer, a slightly reflective glass skin complements the system of solar protection. Roller blinds are also provided inside. Panoramic views toward the Gulf to the east, the port to the south, the city on the west, and the desert on the north are offered on each floor. A planted slope rises toward the lobby and its glass canopy. Inside, an atrium rises to level 27 (112 meters). The architect declares that, "Tall and slim, glittering in its silvery laced silhouette against the skyline, the tower is bound to become a fine landmark on the Doha Corniche."

Der 231 m hohe Turm wurde im Zuge der umfassenden kulturellen Entwicklungspläne unter Scheich Saud Al Thani geplant. Er befindet sich zwischen dem neuen Stadtzentrum und der Corniche auf der Nordseite der Bucht von Doha. Wie die nicht realisierte Tour Sans Fins (Paris, 1989) und die kürzlich fertiggestellte Torre Agbar (Barcelona, 2000–05) hat er einen kreisförmigen Grundriss, wobei die Tragkonstruktion im Bereich der Fassade und nicht im Gebäudekern angeordnet ist. Der Turm misst 45 m im Durchmesser; seine Spitze ist kuppelartig geformt. Schmetterlingsförmige Aluminiumelemente, die »an die geometrische Komplexität der *mashrabiyya* erinnern« sind entsprechend der Himmelsrichtung Teil der Fassade – Richtung Norden nehmen sie 25 % der Fassadenfläche ein, nach Süden 40 % und nach Osten und Westen 60 %. Hinter dieser Schicht schützt eine Haut aus leicht reflektierendem Glas vor zu starker Sonneneinstrahlung. Innenliegende Rollos ergänzen den Sonnenschutz. Alle Geschosse bieten einen Blick auf den Golf, den Hafen im Süden, die Stadt im Westen und die Wüste im Norden. Die Lobby mit einem Glasvordach wird über eine geneigte und bepflanzte Ebene erschlossen. Ein Atrium reicht bis zum 27. Geschoss bzw. bis auf 112 m Höhe. »Hoch und schlank und glitzernd, wie in silbrige Spitze gekleidet, wird der Turm ganz sicher ein Wahrzeichen an der Corniche von Doha werden«, sagt Nouvel.

Cette tour de 231 m de haut fait partie des vastes plans de développement culturel lancés par le cheikh Saoud al-Thani. Elle est située entre le nouveau centre-ville et la Corniche au nord de la baie de Doha. S'appuyant sur des idées mises au point pour sa Tour sans fins (non construite, Paris, 1989), et plus récemment pour la Tour Agbar à Barcelone (2000–05), Nouvel a dessiné un immeuble de plan circulaire dont les éléments structurants sont en périphérie et non le noyau. Ronde comme ses précurseurs, la tour de Doha s'achève par une coupole mesure 45 m de diamètre. Des éléments en aluminium, « rappel de la complexité géométrique des moucharabiehs », sont disposés sur la façade selon une orientation spécifique à chaque partie de l'immeuble : 25 % vers le nord, 40 % vers le sud, 60 % vers l'est et l'ouest. Posée sous cette première strate, une peau de verre légèrement réfléchissante complète le système de protection solaire ainsi que des volets roulants aux fenêtres. De chaque niveau, on bénéficie de vues panoramiques vers le Golfe à l'est, le port au sud, la ville à l'ouest et le désert au nord. Un plan incliné végétalisé s'élève jusqu'au hall d'accueil et son auvent de verre. L'atrium interne mesure 112 m de haut (niveau 27). Pour Jean Nouvel : « Fine et élancée, scintillante dans sa silhouette de dentelle argentée qui se détache sur le panorama urbain, la tour devrait être un des beaux monuments de la Corniche de Doha. »

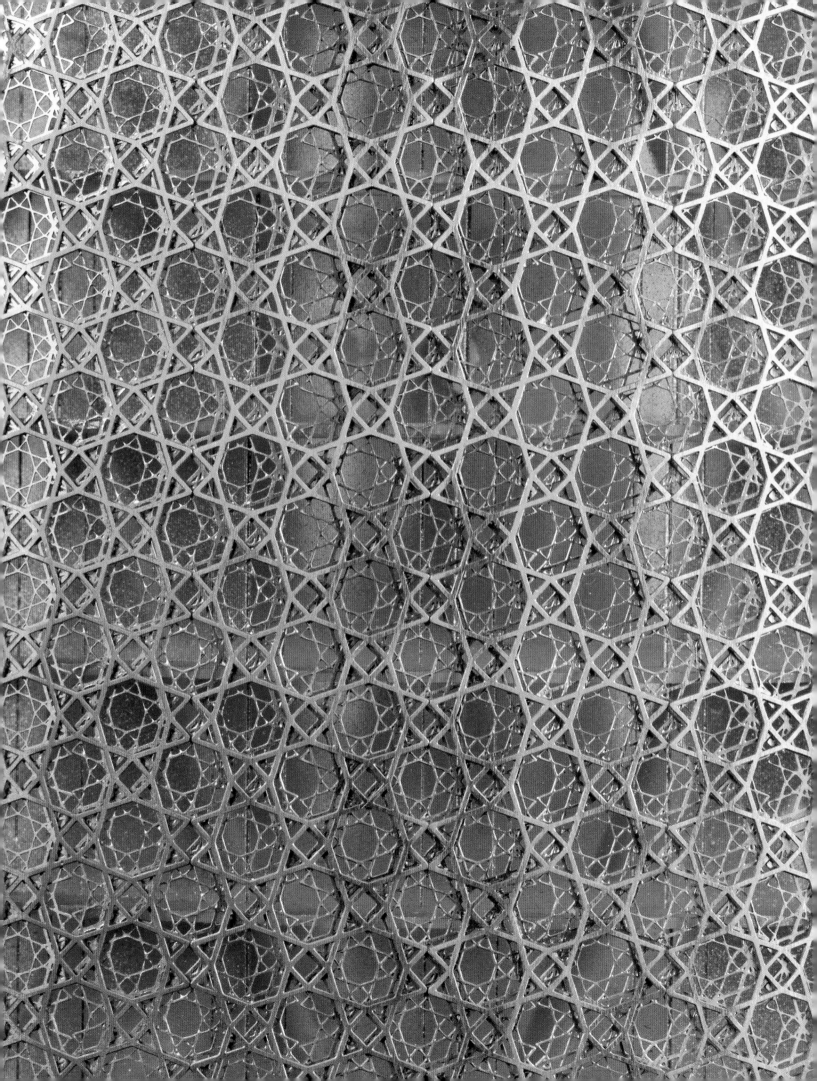

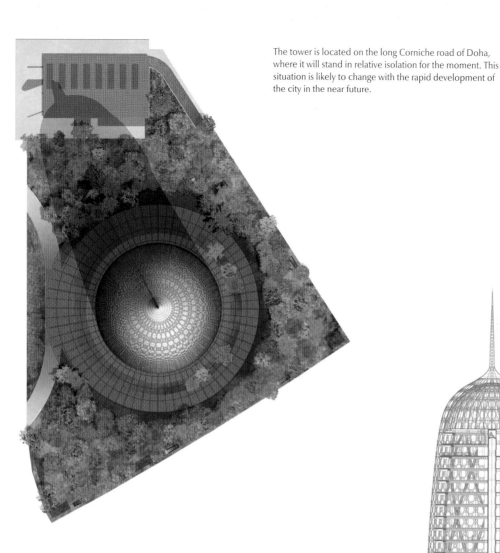

The tower is located on the long Corniche road of Doha, where it will stand in relative isolation for the moment. This situation is likely to change with the rapid development of the city in the near future.

Der Turm an der Corniche von Doha wird dort erst einmal relativ isoliert stehen. Die Situation wird sich aber wahrscheinlich durch die schnelle Entwicklung der Stadt bald ändern.

La tour située le long de la Corniche de Doha se trouve encore relativement isolée, une situation qui changera sans doute avec le rythme du développement urbain prévu un futur proche.

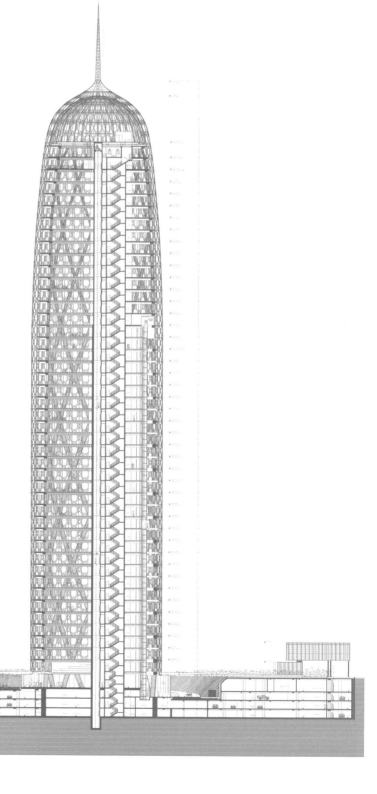

The round, admittedly rather phallic form of the tower is related to other Nouvel projects such as the Agbar Tower in Barcelona.

Die runde, zugegebenermaßen phallische Form des Turms ist mit anderen Projekten von Nouvel, etwa der Torre Agbar in Barcelona, verwandt.

La forme ronde, peut-être assez phallique, de la tour renvoie à d'autres projets de Nouvel comme, par exemple, la tour Agbar à Barcelone.

LOUVRE ABU DHABI
ABU DHABI, UAE
2007-12

ARCHITECT PARTNER: Hala Warde
AREA: 17 000 m²
CLIENT: Tourism Development and Investment
Company of Abu Dhabi (TDIC)
COST: not disclosed
PROJECT MANAGEMENT: Agence Internationale des
Musées de France
PROJECT LEADER: Joseph Tohmé

One of the most prestigious of the new institutions announced early in 2007 for the Saadiyat Island Cultural Complex is Jean Nouvel's Louvre Abu Dhabi. In a move that prompted extensive criticism in France, the French Ministry of Culture and the Louvre Museum agreed to a 30-year association with the Gulf Emirate. Long-term loans from the Louvre, but also from other major French institutions such as the Quai Branly Museum, the Georges Pompidou Center, Musée d'Orsay, Versailles, Guimet and the Rodin Museum, were agreed to as well as "temporary exhibitions to be organized annually in the Louvre Abu Dhabi, to be included in the program of international exhibitions exchanged between major museums worldwide." In return for the participation of the French institution, cash payments and contributions to such projects as the restoration of the Chateau of Fontainebleau in France were agreed to by the authorities of Abu Dhabi. When the project was originally announced in January 2007, Nouvel explained that his design owes much to Saadiyat's natural surroundings. "The island offers a harsh landscape, tempered by its meeting with the channel, a striking image of the aridity of the earth versus the fluidity of the waters. These fire the imagination toward unknown cities buried deep into the sands or sunk under water. These dreamy thoughts have merged into a simple plan of an archaeological field revived as a small city, a cluster of nearly one-row buildings along a leisurely promenade. This micro-city requires a microclimate that would give the visitor a feeling of entering a different world. The building is covered with a large dome, a form common to all civilizations. This one is made of a web of different patterns interlaced into a translucent ceiling that lets a diffuse, magical light come through in the best tradition of great Arabian architecture.

Nouvels Louvre Abu Dhabi ist einer der prestigeträchtigen neuen Kulturbauten im Kulturdistrikt auf Saadiyat, deren Entwürfe Anfang 2007 vorgestellt wurden. Der französische Minister für Kultur und der Louvre waren zuvor darin übereingekommen, eine 30-jährige Partnerschaft mit dem Golfemirat Abu Dhabi einzugehen – und wurden dafür in Frankreich scharf kritisiert. Langfristige Leihgaben vom Louvre, aber auch von anderen großen Museen wie dem Musée du Quai Branly, dem Centre Georges Pompidou, dem Musée d'Orsay, Versailles, dem Musée Guimet und dem Musée Rodin wurden vereinbart, darüber hinaus die Organisation »temporärer Ausstellungen, die jährlich im Louvre Abu Dhabi stattfinden und in das internationale Ausstellungsaustauschprogramm zwischen den großen Museen weltweit einbezogen werden sollen«. Als Gegenleistung für das Engagement des Louvre wird Abu Dhabi dem Louvre eine bestimmte Summe zahlen und Projekte wie z. B. die Instandsetzung von Schloss Fontainebleau unterstützen. Bei der Vorstellung des Projekts erläuterte Nouvel, dass sein Entwurf stark von der na-

türlichen Umgebung der Insel beeinflusst wurde: »Saadiyat ist eine karge Landschaft, die durch den Kanal gezähmt wird – ein starkes Bild für die Trockenheit der Erde im Gegensatz zur Flüssigkeit des Wassers. Dieser Kontrast beflügelt die Vorstellungskraft hin zu unbekannten, tief im Sand vergrabenen oder im Meer versunkenen Städten. Solche träumerischen Gedanken flossen in den einfachen Grundriss eines ›archäologischen Feldes‹ ein, das als kleine Stadt zu neuem Leben erweckt wird – ein Cluster von unterschiedlich großen Gebäuden entlang einer entspannten Fußgängerpromenade. Diese Mikrostadt braucht ein Mikroklima, das dem Besucher das Gefühl gibt, in eine andere Welt einzutauchen. Das Museum wird daher von einer großen flachen Kuppel überdeckt, einer Form, die in allen Kulturkreisen bekannt ist. Diese Kuppel besteht aus einem Netz unterschiedlicher, miteinander verwobener Muster, die eine transluzente Decke bilden, die in bester Tradition arabischer Architektur ein diffuses magisches Licht durchsickern lässt.

Le Louvre Abu Dhabi construit par Jean Nouvel sera l'une des plus prestigieuses institutions nouvelles annoncées début 2007 dans le cadre du complexe culturel de l'île de Saadiyat. Initiative qui a déclenché une importante controverse en France, le ministère de la culture français et le Musée du Louvre ont signé des accords d'association d'une durée de 30 ans avec l'émirat du Golfe. Des prêts d'œuvres à long terme pris dans les collections du Louvre, mais aussi à d'autres grandes institutions françaises comme le Musée du quai Branly, le Centre Georges Pompidou, le Musée d'Orsay, Versailles, les musées Guimet et Rodin sont prévus, ainsi que des « expositions temporaires qui seront organisées chaque année au Louvre Abu Dhabi et incluses dans le programme d'échange d'expositions internationales organisé entre les grands musées du monde ». En retour, des contributions financières et des aides à des projets comme la restauration du château de Fontainebleau seront versées par les autorités d'Abu Dhabi. À l'annonce du projet en janvier 2007, Nouvel avait expliqué que son projet devait beaucoup à l'environnement naturel de Saadiyat. « L'île présente un paysage rude tempéré par sa rencontre avec le canal, image frappante de l'aridité de la terre versus la fluidité des eaux. Ces considérations rêveuses ont abouti à un plan simple de champ de fouilles archéologiques réanimé en une petite ville, un regroupement de constructions le long d'une agréable promenade. Cette microcité requiert un microclimat qui donnera au visiteur le sentiment de pénétrer dans un univers différent. Les constructions seront recouvertes d'une vaste coupole, forme commune à toutes les civilisations. Celle-ci se composera d'un réseau de différents motifs entrelacés dans un plafond translucide qui laissera passer une lumière diffuse et magique dans la meilleure tradition de la grande architecture arabe.

The principle of the design is to create a gigantic curved dome over the actual museum facilities, with irregular openings to let in a complex pattern of daylight.

Grundgedanke des Entwurfs ist die riesige Kuppel, die die Museumseinrichtungen zusammenfasst. Unregelmäßige kleine Ausschnitte in der Kuppel schaffen komplexe Lichtmuster.

Le principe de ce projet est la création d'une gigantesque coupole posée au-dessus des diverses installations muséales. Des ouvertures irrégulières créent des effets d'éclairage complexes.

Interior space will be animated in the day by the changing sunlight patterns generated by the openings in the covering dome.

Kleine Ausschnitte in der Kuppel erzeugen tagsüber sich verändernde Lichtmuster, die die Innenräume beleben.

L'espace intérieur sera animé de jour par les modifications de l'éclairage naturel pénétrant par les ouvertures de la coupole

13

OMA / REM KOHLHAAS

OFFICE FOR METROPOLITAN ARCHITECTURE (OMA)
Heer Bokelweg 149
3032 AD Rotterdam
The Netherlands

Tel: +31 10 243 8200
Fax: +31 10 243 8202
e-mail: office@oma.nl
Web: http://www.oma.nl

Rem Koolhaas created the **OFFICE FOR METROPOLITAN ARCHITECTURE** in 1975, together with Elia and Zoe Zenghelis and Madelon Vriesendorp. Born in Rotterdam in 1944, Koolhaas tried his hand as a journalist for the *Haagse Post* and as a screenwriter, before studying at the Architectural Association in London. He became well known after the 1978 publication of his book *Delirious New York*. OMA is led today by six partners: Rem Koolhaas, Ole Scheeren, Ellen van Loon, Reinier de Graaf, Floris Alkemade, and Managing Director Victor van der Chijs. Their built work includes a group of apartments at Nexus World, Fukuoka, Japan (1991), and the Villa dall'Ava, Saint-Cloud, France (1985–91). Koolhaas was named head architect of the Euralille project in Lille, France, in 1988, and has worked on a design for the new Jussieu University Library in Paris. His 1400-page book S,M,L,XL (Monacelli Press, 1995) has more than fulfilled his promise as an influential writer. He won the 2000 Pritzker Prize and the 2003 Praemium Imperiale Award for architecture. More recent work of OMA includes a house in Bordeaux, France (1998); the campus center at the Illinois Institute of Technology; the new Dutch Embassy in Berlin, Germany; as well as the Guggenheim Las Vegas and Prada boutiques in New York and Los Angeles. OMA completed the Seattle Public Library in 2004, and participated in the Samsung Museum of Art (Leeum) in Seoul, Korea, with Mario Botta and Jean Nouvel. Current work includes OMA's largest project ever: the 575 000-square-meter Headquarters and Cultural Center for China Central Television (CCTV) in Beijing; a master plan for the White City area of London; a harbor redevelopment in Riga, Latvia, including a contemporary art museum; the Cordoba Congress Center in Spain; the redevelopment of the Mercati Generali in Rome, Italy; the Zeche Zollverein Historical Museum and master plan in Essen, Germany; the new head office of Rothschild Bank in London; a mixed-use development project in Seoul, Korea; and several projects in The Netherlands, such as the city centre of Almere and the MAB/OVG multiuse towers in Rotterdam. In the Middle East, OMA is working on two master plans in Dubai, a master plan in Kuwait and another in Ras-Al-Khaimah. OMA New York is currently working on a mixed-use development in Jersey City's arts district; and for Cornell University in Ithaca, OMA is designing the new Millstein Hall.

RAK CONVENTION EXHIBITION CENTER RAS AL KHAIMAH, UAE 2006-

PARTNERS IN CHARGE: OMA/Rem Koolhaas,
Reinier de Graaf
CLIENT: RAK Investment Authority
COST: not disclosed
TEAM: Samir Bantal, Daniele de Benedictis,
Anne-Sophie Bernard, Philippe Braun, Adam Frampton,
Martin Galovsky, Beth Hughes, Pieter Janssen, Ravi
Kamisetti, Bin Kim, Barend Koolhaas, So Jung Lee, Mirai
Morita, Charles-Antoine Perreault, Ian Robertson

Ras Al Khaimah is the northernmost of the seven United Arab Emirates, located near Oman on the Arabian Peninsula. The recorded history of the city, formerly called Julfar, goes back to the eighth century A. D., and present population numbers about 105 000 people. An unusual aspect of this new convention and exhibition center, including hotels, offices, residential space, retail and restaurants, is that all of its primary functions are situated in a giant sphere. A low-rise building adjacent to this very large globe will appear to "hover" above the ground and will contain additional retail and hotel space. Confronted with the race to create extravagant shapes in new construction, particularly in the United Arab Emirates, OMA and Rem Koolhaas have proposed to confront this issue "not through the creation of the next bizarre image, but through a return to pure form." The "perfectly autonomous" shapes of the RAK Convention and Exhibition Center will be connected to the city of Ras Al Khaimah through a new road network, making it an integral part of the emerging urban landscape. The RAK Center was originally designed to be the outstanding complex located at the edge of the ambitious 37 million-square-meter Gateway project being undertaken by RAK Investment Authority, intended to house 150 000 people. OMA did not win the competition for this project, although the design may move forward elsewhere. The architects conclude, "In spite of their apparent simplicity, the sphere and the bar could come to represent a milestone in the construction of the new RAK and provide it with a powerful universal symbol: Western and Eastern, futuristic and primordial, contemporary and timeless."

Ras al-Khaima ist das nördlichste der sieben Vereinigten Arabischen Emirate und grenzt an Oman. Die überlieferte Geschichte der Hauptstadt Ras al-Khaima, das frühere Julfar, reicht bis ins 8. Jahrhundert n. Chr. zurück. Derzeit hat die Stadt ca. 105 000 Einwohner. Alle wesentlichen Funktionen des neuen Kongress- und Ausstellungszentrums, das Hotels, Büros, Wohnungen, Läden und Restaurants umfasst, sind in einer gigantischen Kugel untergebracht. Ein flaches Gebäude, das neben der Kugel zu schweben scheint, enthält weitere Laden- und Hotelflächen. In den Vereinigten Emiraten, wo ein besonders harter Wettkampf um immer extravagantere Formen für neue Bauvorhaben herrscht, reagierten OMA/Rem Koolhaas »nicht mit einem weiteren bizarren Bild, sondern mit einer Rückkehr zur reinen Form«. Die »vollkommen autonomen« Baukörper des RAK sollen mit Ras al-Khaima durch ein neues Straßennetz verbunden und so zu einem Bestandteil der wachsenden Stadtlandschaft werden. Das Kongress- und Ausstellungszentrum wird das architektonische Highlight am Rand der ehrgeizigen, 37 Millionen m² großen Gateway City sein, die von RAK Investment Authority entwickelt wird und in der später einmal 150 000 Menschen leben sollen. Auch wenn OMA den Wettbewerb zu diesem Projekt nicht gewonnen hat, wird das Design sicherlich an einem anderen Ort umgesetzt. Die Architekten folgern: »Trotz ihrer einfachen Formen könnten die Kugel und der Riegel ein Meilenstein bei der Realisierung des neuen Ras al-Khaima werden; ein kraftvolles, universales Symbol – dem Westen und Osten zugehörig, futuristisch und ursprünglich, zeitgenössisch und zeitlos.«

Près d'Oman, l'émirat de Ras el Khaïmah est le plus septentrional des sept EAU. L'histoire connue de la ville, jadis appelée Julfar, remonte au VIIIe siècle. Sa population s'élève à environ 105 000 habitants. Un aspect inhabituel de ce nouveau centre de congrès et d'expositions qui comprend également des hôtels, des bureaux, des appartements, des commerces et des restaurants est le regroupement de ses fonctions principales dans une gigantesque sphère. Un bâtiment bas adjacent qui donne l'impression de « flotter » au-dessus du sol contiendra d'autres boutiques et un hôtel. Confrontés à la course aux formes extravagantes en particulier dans les EAU, l'agence OMA et Rem Koolhaas se sont proposé d'y participer « pas par la création d'une image bizarre de plus, mais par un retour à la forme pure ». Ce centre « parfaitement autonome » sera connecté à la ville de Ras el Khaïmah par un nouveau réseau routier qui l'intègre à un grand plan d'urbanisation en cours. Équipement remarquable, il sera en effet situé en bordure du projet « Gateway » de 37 millions m² mis en œuvre par RAK Investment Authority et qui devrait accueillir 150 000 personnes. Pour les architectes : « Malgré leur simplicité apparente, la sphère et la barre pourraient représenter une étape dans la reconstruction de la ville en lui offrant un symbole universel puissant : occidental et oriental, futuriste et originel, contemporain et intemporel. »

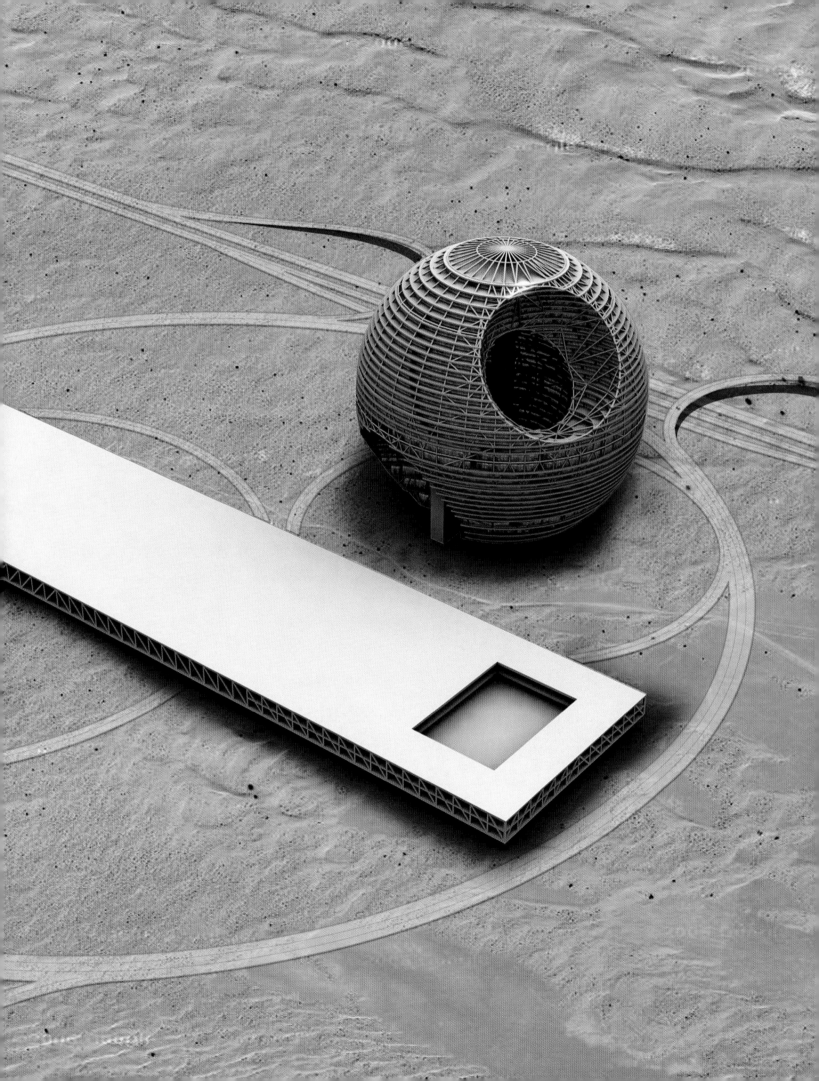

The main sphere of the complex is a mega-structure with circular voids. Set at the periphery of the large Gateway City development, the iconic complex will surely be one of the most unexpected new structures in a region known for its spectacular projects.

Der Kugelbau ist eine Megastruktur mit eingeschnittenen runden Hohlräumen. Der markante Komplex an der Peripherie des großen Entwicklungsgebiets Gateway City wird gewiss einer der spektakulärsten Bauten in der ohnehin für ihre sensationellen Projekte bekannten Region sein.

La sphère principale est une mégastructure découpée de grands vides circulaires. Implanté à la périphérie de l'énorme projet de développement de Gateway City, ce complexe à la forte image sera certainement l'une des constructions les plus surprenantes d'une région déjà connue pour ses réalisations spectaculaires.

The spherical form will be used to generate unexpected and spectacular interior spaces. Plans for the buildings (below) give an idea of its complexity.

Die sphärische Form sorgt für überraschende und spektakuläre Innenräume. Die Grundrisse unten vermitteln eine Vorstellung von der Komplexität des Gebäudes.

La forme sphérique générera des volumes intérieurs étonnants. Les plans ci-dessous donnent une idée de la complexité du projet.

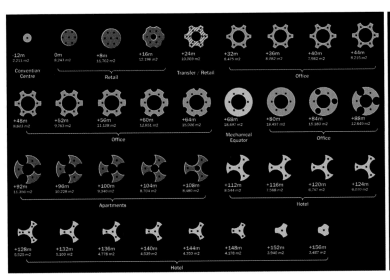

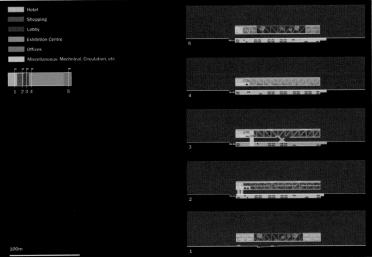

Images that bring to mind some science-fiction films suggest that the RAK Center will indeed be something of a world unto itself, almost as though it had landed in this location like a space craft.

An Science-Fiction-Filme erinnernde Bilder machen deutlich, dass das RAK Center eine Welt für sich sein wird. Es wirkt, als wäre es wie ein Raumschiff an seinem Standort gelandet.

Des images rappellent certains films de science-fiction laissent imaginer que le RAK Center, vaisseau spatial posé dans le désert, constituera une sorte d'univers en soi.

PORSCHE DESIGN BUILDINGS DUBAI, UAE 2007-09

PARTNERS IN CHARGE: OMA/Rem Kohlhaas, Fernando Donis
AREA: 85 000 m² (office tower); 30 000 m² (residential tower)
CLIENT: Dubai Properties COST: not disclosed
Joint project with Porsche Design Studio, part of Porsche Lizenz-
und Handelsgesellschaft mbH & Co. KG (Porsche Design Group)

Announced in October 2006, this project involves two towers, one residential and the other for offices, set next to each other on the waterfront in the Dubai Business Bay area. The Business Bay area, with a total floor space of 6.4 million square meters, has been developed by Dubai Properties. Due to be finished in 2009, this will be the first OMA project completed in the Middle East. The 20-story office building will include retail and recreational spaces, while the 80-meter residential building is due to be built above a sunken plaza with further retail spaces and cafés. The German real-estate agents Engel & Völkers of Hamburg are marketing both the apartments and the office spaces. The designs naturally take into account the climate conditions in Dubai. Thus the office tower "is framed by side wings and an overlap to create its own shadow, thereby protecting the tower from sunlight and reducing the need for air conditioning." Reflective glass is used in the large central panel of this cube-shaped design. The round residential building will have a full-height atrium designed to make use of natural air circulation and to bring daylight into the core of the structure. In this joint venture with Porsche Design Studio from Germany, OMA is in charge of design for both buildings, and Porsche will have "a consulting role for the outside architecture and be in charge of designing public areas such as the lobby, restaurants and passenger lifts." Furniture, lighting, and kitchens designed by Porsche can be provided to residents on their request.

Das im Oktober 2006 vorgestellte Projekt besteht aus zwei Türmen – einem Wohn- und einem Bürohochhaus –, die nebeneinander am Meer in der Dubai Business Bay stehen. Die Business Bay mit einer Gesamtfläche von 6,4 Millionen m² wird von der Immobiliengesellschaft Dubai Properties entwickelt. 2009 sollen die Türme fertiggestellt sein und werden dann die ersten von OMA im Nahen Osten realisierten Bauten sein. In dem 20-geschossigen Bürohaus sind neben Büros Läden sowie Freizeiteinrichtungen untergebracht. Auch in dem 80 m hohen Wohnhochhaus, das über einer abgesenkten Plaza steht, wird es Einkaufsflächen und Cafés geben. Das deutsche Maklerbüro Engel & Völkers mit Sitz in Hamburg vermarktet sowohl die Wohnungen als auch die Büroflächen. Natürlich nehmen die Gebäude auf die klimatischen Bedingungen in Dubai Rücksicht: Der Büroturm wird »von Seitenteilen und einem Dachüberstand gerahmt und erzeugt so seinen eigenen Schatten, der das Haus vor der Sonne schützt und damit den Klimatisierungsbedarf reduziert«. Der große mittlere Bereich der Fassade des quaderförmigen Gebäudes ist mit Reflexionsglas ausgestattet. Um die natürliche Luftzirkulation zu nutzen und Tageslicht ins Innere des Gebäudes zu bringen, gibt es in der Mitte des runden Wohnturms ein Atrium, das über die gesamte Höhe des Hauses reicht. OMA kooperiert bei diesem Projekt mit dem Porsche Design Studio, Deutschland. Dabei zeichnet OMA für den Entwurf der beiden Gebäude verantwortlich, Porsche »ist bei der Außenarchitektur beratend tätig und für die Gestaltung der öffentlichen Bereiche – etwa die Lobby, die Restaurants und Personenaufzüge – zuständig«. Auf Wunsch der Bewohner können die Apartments mit Möbeln, Beleuchtungskörpern und Küchen von Porsche Design ausgestattet werden.

Annoncé en octobre 2006, ce projet comprend deux tours voisines, une d'appartements, l'autre de bureaux, implantées sur le front de mer de la Business Bay à Dubaï, une zone de 6,4 millions de m² aménagés par Dubai Properties. Prévu pour 2009, ce sera le premier projet achevé par OMA au Moyen-Orient. La tour de bureaux de 20 étages contiendra également des espaces commerciaux et de loisirs, et l'immeuble résidentiel de 80 m de haut dominant une place en creux, des commerces et des cafés. L'agence immobilière de Hambourg, Engel & Völkers, commercialise l'ensemble. Ces deux projets prennent bien entendu en compte les conditions climatiques. Ainsi la tour de bureaux « est encadrée par les ailes latérales et un recouvrement qui crée de l'ombre, protège la tour de la lumière solaire et réduit les besoins de climatisation ». Un verre réfléchissant est utilisé dans la vaste partie centrale de ce projet en forme de cube. L'immeuble résidentiel circulaire possèdera un atrium qui occupera toute sa hauteur pour favoriser la circulation de l'air naturel et apporter la lumière du jour au cœur de la structure. Dans cette opération menée en commun avec Porsche Design Studio, l'agence OMA a été chargée de la conception des deux immeubles, et Porsche d'un « rôle de consultant sur l'extérieur de l'architecture et la conception des espaces publics, dont les halls d'accueil, les restaurants et les ascenseurs ». Le mobilier, l'éclairage et les cuisines conçus par Porsche peuvent être fournis aux résidants sur demande.

The sophistication of the interior design will be carefully related to the architecture, making this complex one of the most prestigious addresses of Dubai.

Die anspruchsvolle Innenraumgestaltung ist sorgfältig auf die Architektur bezogen und macht diesen Gebäudekomplex zu einer der prestigeträchtigsten Adressen in Dubai.

La sophistication de l'architecture intérieure sera traitée dans le même esprit que l'architecture globale pour faire de ce complexe l'une des plus prestigieuses adresses de Dubaï.

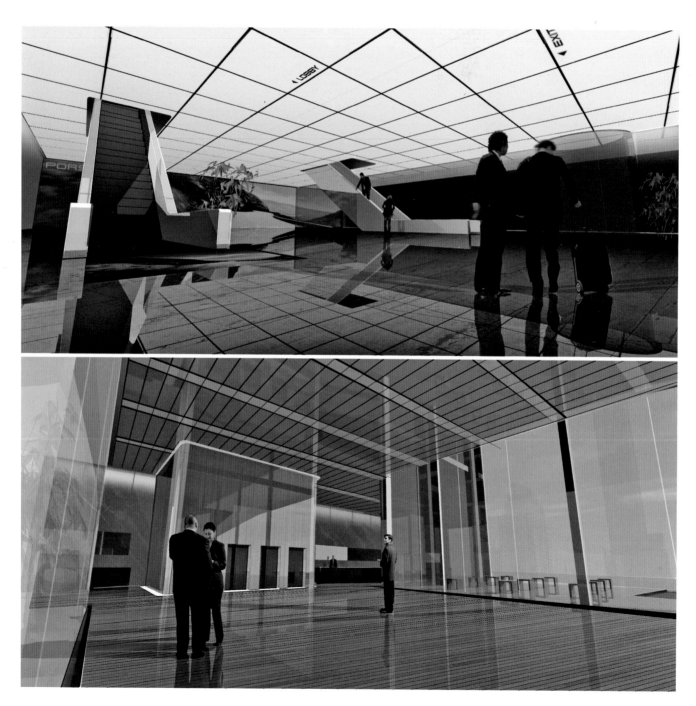

The monolithic appearance of the architectural forms is emphasized in this night perspective, with ribbed openings giving some idea of the activity within the buildings.

Die Nachtansicht betont die monolithische Erscheinung der Baukörper. Rippenartig überdeckte Glasfassaden lassen die Aktivitäten im Inneren des Gebäudes erahnen.

L'aspect monolithique des formes architecturales est mis en valeur dans cette perspective nocturne. Les ouvertures en nervures laissent entrevoir l'activité interne.

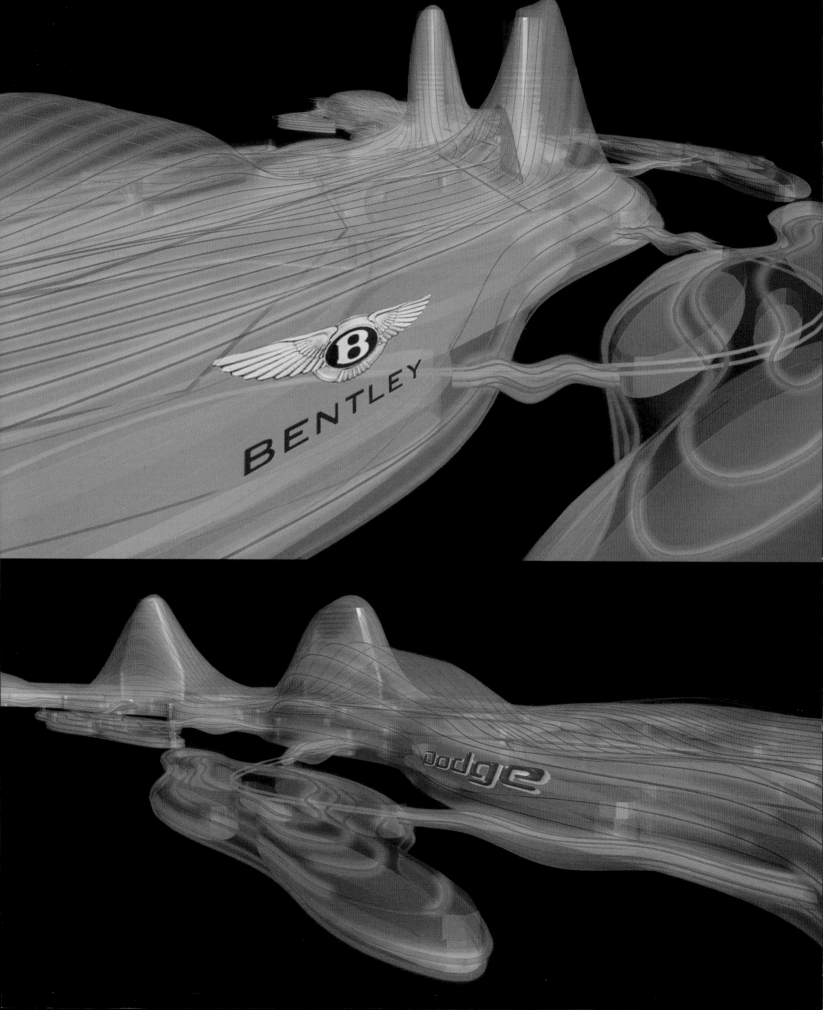

14

ONL

ONL
Essenburgsingel 94c
3022 EG Rotterdam
The Netherlands

Tel: +31 10 244 7039
Fax +31 10 244 7041
e-mail: oosterhuis@oosterhuis.nl
Web: www.oosterhuis.nl

ONL is described as a "multidisciplinary architectural firm where architects, visual artists, web designers and programmers work together and join forces." Kas Oosterhuis was born in Amersfoort in 1951. He studied architecture at the Technical University in Delft (1970–79) and was a Unit Master at the AA in London (1987–89). He has been a Professor at the Technical University in Delft since 2000. He is a member of the board of the Witte de With Museum in Rotterdam. He has built the Multimedia Pavilion, North Holland Floriade (2000–01); Headquarters for True Colors, Utrecht (2000–01); and the Salt Water Pavilion, Neeltje Jans, Zeeland (1994–97). Ilona Lénárd is the other Principal of ONL [Oosterhuis_Lénárd]. A visual artist, she was born in Hungary, and lived and worked in the Atelier Theo van Doesburg in Meudon, France (1988–89). She has worked with Kas Oosterhuis on various projects that involve a fusion of art and architecture. One notable recent project is the WTC 911 project that proposes a "self-executable and programmable hi-res building which reconfigures its shape, content and character during one year of its life cycle." Other recent work includes: 9 Variomatic catalogue houses, Deventer (2000); TT monument, Assen (with Ilona Lénárd, 2000); and an Acoustic Barrier, Leidsche Rijn, Utrecht (2002). ONL has recently worked on a number of other ventures including sophisticated projects that use engineering or game software to develop new types of space. ONL's "Protospace" project at the TU Delft involves creating virtual, interactive architecture. Their Acoustic Barrier, Ekris Showroom, and Hessing Cockpit (Leidsche Rijn Utrecht, 2000–05) developed the theme of a combined automotive sales facility and sound barrier. Their Flyotel in Dubai is in the design phase.

AUTOMOTIVE COMPLEX
ABU DHABI, UAE
2006-

FLOOR AREA: 1.5 million m²
CLIENT: not disclosed COST: not disclosed
DESIGN TEAM: Kas Oosterhuis, Ilona Lénárd,
Gijs Joosen, Cas Aalbers, Sander Boer,
Thomas Jaskiewicz, Dieter Vandoren,
Barbara Janssen, Henrike Michler, Eirini Logara,
Han Feng, Brenda Vonk Noordegraaf

This master plan for an automotive sales complex covers an area of more than six square kilometers. The Complex itself is a 2.5-kilometer-long terminal with "satellites" and "capsules" for the display and sale of different automobile brands in both new and used models. Major brands will have repair garages as part of the site. A car museum, style center, design academy and children's car track, food courts, and other retail spaces are also part of the program, as are a hotel, conference room and offices. Test-driving tracks for both fast cars and SUVs are planned. Kas Oosterhuis explains, "The theme chosen for the development of the Automotive Complex is speed and friction. People are driving cars, buying cars, and living their life in and around cars. The culture of cars is also the culture of driving fast, the culture of speed. And the culture of people with cars is also the culture of friction: the friction of the tires on the asphalt, the friction of the cars in the traffic flow, the resistance of the wheels and springs while driving on the rocky riverbeds of the wadis, and the delicate grip of the flattened tires on the soft sand dunes while dune bashing. Everyone likes to go fast, but reality balances out the speed because of the friction. The theme of speed and friction can be expanded beyond the realm of cars into the realm of transportation at large. The friction of the air for fast airplanes, the friction of the water for speedboats." The speed-influenced architecture designed on computers by ONL for this Automotive Complex develops out of the stunning forms of the Acoustic Barrier they recently completed in The Netherlands.

Der Masterplan für einen Automobilverkaufskomplex umfasst eine Fläche von 6 km². Das Verkaufsgebäude selbst ist ein 2,5 km langer Terminal, an den »Satelliten« und »Raumkapseln« für die Präsentation und den Verkauf verschiedener Automarken angehängt werden. Sowohl neue Modelle als auch Gebrauchtwagen können in dem Komplex erworben werden; daneben unterhalten die großen Autohersteller Werkstätten. Es gibt ein Automuseum, ein Style Center, eine Design-Akademie, eine Rennstrecke für Kinder, Gastronomieangebote sowie weitere Verkaufsflächen, ferner ein Hotel, Konferenzsäle und Büros. Auch Teststrecken für schnelle Wagen und Geländewagen sind vorhanden. Kas Oosterhuis erläutert: »Die Themen für den Automotive Complex lauten Geschwindigkeit und Reibung. Menschen fahren Autos, sie kaufen Autos, sie leben ihr Leben in Autos und in Abhängigkeit von Autos. Die Autokultur ist auch eine Kultur des Schnellfahrens, eine Kultur der Geschwindigkeit, gleichzeitig ist sie aber auch eine ›Kultur‹ der Reibung: die Reibung der Reifen auf dem Asphalt, die Stockungen im Verkehrsfluss, der Widerstand der Räder und der Federung, wenn man im steinigen Flussbett der Wadi fährt, und der feine Griff der Reifen, aus denen Luft abgelassen wurde, um auf den weichen Sanddünen zu fahren. Jeder fährt gern schnell, in der Realität wird die Geschwindigkeit jedoch durch die Reibung ausgeglichen. Von der Welt des Autos können die Themen Geschwindigkeit und Reibung in den Bereich des Transports im Allgemeinen erweitert werden. Der Reibungswiderstand der Luft beim Fliegen, der Reibungswiderstand des Wassers beim Speedboatfahren.« ONL entwickelte die von Geschwindigkeit inspirierte und computergenerierte Architektur für den Automotive Complex aus der eindrucksvollen Form der kürzlich in den Niederlanden fertiggestellten »Acoustic Barrier«.

Ce plan d'aménagement d'un centre de distribution automobile couvre une surface de plus de 6 km². Le complexe lui-même est un « terminal » de 2,5 km de long sur lequel viennent se greffer des « satellites » ou « capsules » pour l'exposition et la vente de modèles, aussi bien neufs que d'occasion, de diverses marques automobiles. Les plus importantes disposeront également d'ateliers de réparation sur le site. Un musée de l'automobile, un centre de style, une école de design et une piste de voitures d'enfants, des zones de restaurations et autres espaces commerciaux font également partie du programme ainsi qu'un hôtel, des salles de conférences et des bureaux. Des pistes d'essai pour les voitures de sport et les SUV (Sport Utility Vehicles, autrement dit, des 4 x 4) sont prévues. Pour Kas Oosterhuis : « Le thème choisi pour le développement de ce complexe est celui de la vitesse et de la friction. Les gens conduisent des voitures, achètent des voitures et vivent dans et parmi les voitures. La culture des voitures est aussi celle de la conduite rapide, de la vitesse. Et la culture des rapports entre ces gens et ces voitures est aussi celle de la friction : la friction des pneus sur l'asphalte, la friction des voitures dans le flux de la circulation, la résistance des roues et des amortisseurs dans le lit rocheux des *wadi* (vallées) et l'adhérence difficile des pneus dégonflés sur les dunes de sable lors des balades dans le désert. Tout le monde aime aller vite, mais la réalité va à l'encontre de la vitesse du fait de la friction. Le thème de la vitesse et de la friction peut se développer au-delà du domaine de la voiture, jusque dans les transports en général. La friction de l'air pour les avions rapides, la friction de l'eau sur les hors-bords. » Cette architecture, influencée par la vitesse et conçue par ordinateur, est issue des formes étonnantes de la « Barrière acoustique » que l'agence a récemment réalisée aux Pays-Bas.

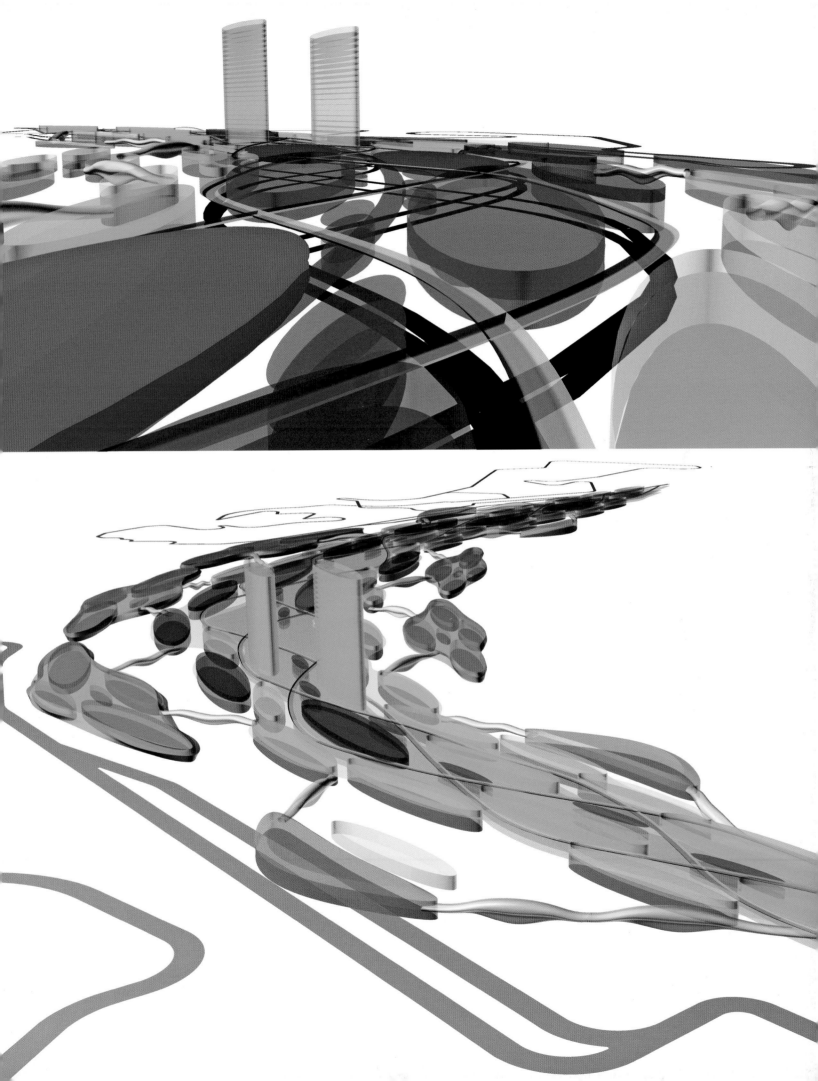

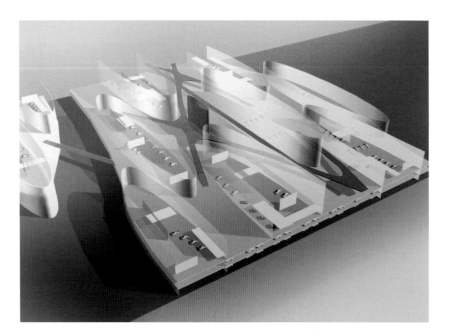

ONL's computer-generated designs suggest a flowing, spectacular design, carried over into the interior spaces.

ONLs computergenerierte Zeichnungen zeigen fließende, spektakuläre Gebäude, deren Innenräume die gleiche Sprache sprechen.

Les images d'ONL générées par ordinateur suggèrent une impression de flux qui se retrouve dans les volumes intérieurs.

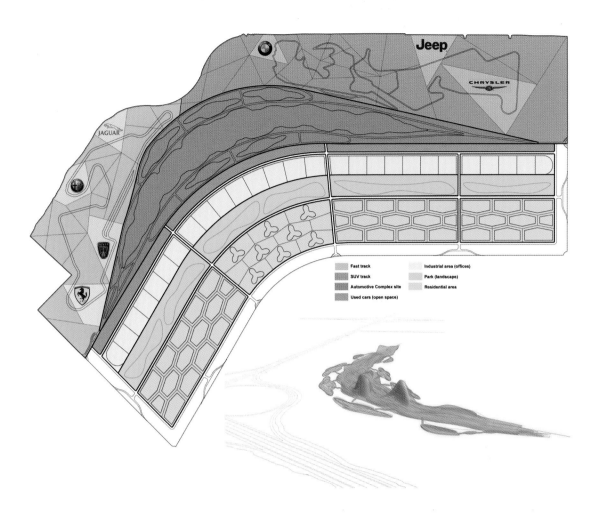

Like ONL's Acoustic Barrier, Ekris Showroom, and Hessing Cockpit (Leidsche Rijn Utrecht, 2000–05), this complex places automobiles in the forefront and adapts a complex, curving design.

Wie bei ONLs »Acoustic Barrier«, dem Ekris-Ausstellungsraum und dem Hessing Cockpit (Leidsche Rijn, Utrecht, 2000–05) steht das Automobil bei den komplexen, kurvig geformten Gebäuden im Mittelpunkt.

Comme dans la Barrière acoustique, le showroom Ekris et le Hessing Cockpit réalisés par ONL (Leidsche Rijn Utrecht, 2000–05), ce complexe met l'automobile au premier plan et adopte un profil complexe tout en courbes.

MANHAL OASIS
ABU DHABI, UAE
2006 -

CLIENT: not disclosed
COST: not disclosed
DESIGN TEAM: Kas Oosterhuis, Ilona Lénárd,
Gijs Joosen, Tomasz Jaskiewicz,
Rafal Seeman, Michal Gorczyncki, Lidia Badarnah,
Rena Logara, Sathish Kumar,
Tomasz Sachanowicz, Jan Gasparik

This is a second master plan designed by ONL for the UAE. It is conceived as a "destination city" with three major attractions: a Cultural Gate" with two museums and the "Xperience Landmark Structure"; a South East Gate with a shopping mall and wellness center; and a Downtown and Souk district with four 60-story, 300-meter-high towers. One pair of these connected structures would be clad in greenish glass, and the other in bluish glass, symbolizing their contrasting residential and office functions. The gates lead to a city oasis with trees from a former plantation on the site. Educational buildings and indoor sports facilities are located at the edge of this oasis. The architects were asked to preserve as much as possible of the plantation, which includes the remains of a royal palace. A bit further from the center, four series of 30-story mixed-use towers, including residential and office space, are located. The project is intended for 50 000 residents and a further 50 000 workers. Interested in computer games, Kas Oosterhuis writes, "The initial condition of the master plan development is like a board game where two teams of players are neatly arranged along the opposite long sides of the site. ONL has transformed the board game into an interwoven mixed-use urban area, where the players have made several moves and have become interlaced in a complex web of relations." The groups of towers of two different heights form the most visible aspect of the skyline of this new city. Oosterhuis, referring to an exhibition held at the Pompidou Center in Paris on the relationship of computer-driven design and construction (Non-Standard Architecture), says, "ONL has chosen the new language of non-standard architecture for the Downtown area to become a symbol for the 21st century, a symbol for a new world order where Arabic culture plays an equally important role as Atlantic Western culture and Pacific Asian culture."

Der Masterplan ist der zweite, den ONL für die Vereinigten Arabischen Emirate erarbeitet hat. Drei Hauptattraktionen bestimmen den Entwurf für die Stadt, die ein Anziehungspunkt für Touristen sein soll: das Cultural Gate mit zwei Museen und dem Xperience-Gebäude als Wahrzeichen, das South East Gate mit einem Einkaufszentrum und Wellnesscenter sowie ein Downtown- und Souk-Distrikt mit vier 60-geschossigen, 300 m hohen Türmen. Zwei dieser miteinander verbundenen Gebäude sind in grünliches Glas gekleidet, zwei in bläuliches. Die Farben symbolisieren die unterschiedlichen Nutzungen als Wohn- bzw. Bürogebäude. Die Torgebäude führen zu einer Oase, deren Baumbestand von einer Plantage stammt, die sich früher hier befand. Schulgebäude und Indoor-Sporteinrichtungen säumen den Rand der Oase. Die Architekten wurden aufgefordert, so viel wie möglich von der Plantage, in der sich auch Reste eines königlichen Palastes finden, zu erhalten. Etwas weiter vom Zentrum entfernt stehen vier Reihen 30-geschossiger Türme für Wohn- und Büronutzung. Geplant ist die Stadt für 50 000 Einwohner und weitere 50 000 Angestellte. Der an Computerspielen interessierte Oosterhuis schreibt: »Bei der Entwicklung des Masterplans gingen wir von der Idee eines Spielbretts aus: Dabei sitzen sich zwei Teams ordentlich entlang der Längsseiten des Grundstücks gegenüber. ONL hat das Brettspiel in ein städtisches Gebiet mit einer ineinander verwobenen Mischnutzung verwandelt. Die Spieler haben verschiedene Züge gemacht und sind nun in einem komplexen Beziehungsgeflecht miteinander verbunden.« Die zentrale Hochhausgruppe mit Türmen in zwei Höhen prägt die Skyline der neuen Stadt. Oosterhuis bezieht sich auf die Ausstellung »Non-Standard Architecture« im Centre Georges Pompidou in Paris, die die Beziehung von am Computer generierten Entwürfen und die computergestützte Herstellung dieser Gebäude thematisierte, und sagt: »ONL hat sich im Zentrum der Stadt für die Sprache der ›Non-Standard Architecture‹ entschieden, um sie zu einem Symbol des 21. Jahrhunderts zu machen, einem Symbol für eine neue Weltordnung, in der die arabische Kultur eine genauso wichtige Rolle wie die westliche und die asiatische Kultur spielt.«

Il s'agit du second plan directeur d'urbanisme conçu par ONL pour les EAU. Cette « oasis » sera une « ville de destination » dotée de trois attractions majeures : une « Culture Gate » comprenant deux musées et une structure monumentale appelée « Xperience », une « South East Gate » équipée d'un centre commercial et d'installations sportives, et un quartier central avec Souk constitué de quatre tours de 60 niveaux et 300 m de haut. Deux de ces tours reliées entre elles seront habillées de verre de couleur verte, et une troisième de verre bleuâtre pour souligner la différence de leur fonction : bureaux et résidences. Les portes ouvrent sur une cité-oasis qui profite des arbres déjà existants. Les bâtiments pour l'éducation et les sports d'intérieur sont situés en bordure. Les architectes devaient respecter autant que possible les plantations et les vestiges d'un palais royal. À une certaine distance du centre, s'élèveront quatre ensembles de tours mixtes de 30 niveaux (bureaux et logements). Le projet devrait accueillir 50 000 résidents et 50 000 postes de travail. Intéressé par les jeux sur ordinateur, Kas Oosterhuis écrit : « L'état initial du plan directeur de développement est comme un jeu d'échec où deux équipes de joueurs sont disposées en ordre de bataille, face-à-face. ONL a transformé ce jeu en zone urbaine à usages mixtes imbriqués, dans laquelle les joueurs ont effectué divers mouvements et se trouvent maintenant dans un réseau complexe de relations. » Ces groupes de tours de différentes hauteurs constituent l'aspect le plus visible du panorama de cette ville nouvelle. Oosterhuis, qui se réfère à une exposition organisée au Centre Pompidou à Paris sur les relations entre la conception assistée par ordinateur et la construction (« Architecture Non Standar »), précise enfin : « ONL a choisi le nouveau langage de l'architecture non standard pour ce centre qui doit devenir un symbole du XXIe siècle, le symbole d'un nouvel ordre mondial dans lequel la culture arabe jouera une rôle aussi important que la culture occidentale atlantique et la culture asiatique du Pacifique. »

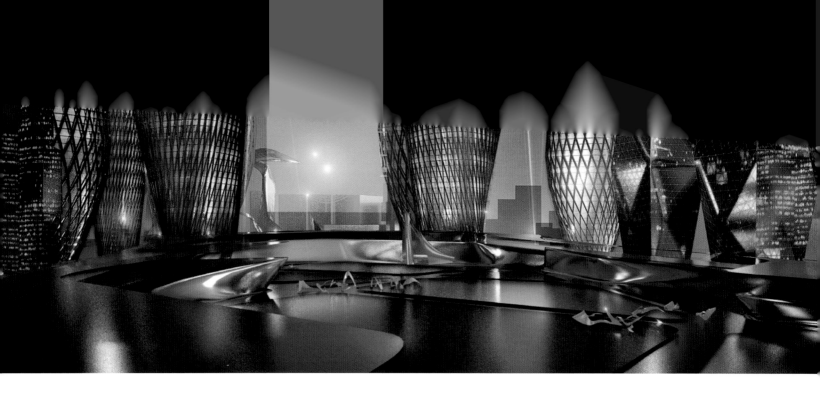

The plan proposed by ONL involves what might be compared to a forest of unusually shaped towers, varying from folded plane designs to rounded tree-like buildings.

Der von ONL vorgeschlagene Plan zeigt eine Art Wald aus ungewöhnlich geformten Türmen, die Formen variieren zwischen gefalteten, geraden Entwürfen und gerundeten, baumartigen Gebäuden.

Le plan proposé par ONL évoque une forêt de tours toutes différentes, dont les formes vont du plan replié à des évocations d'arbres.

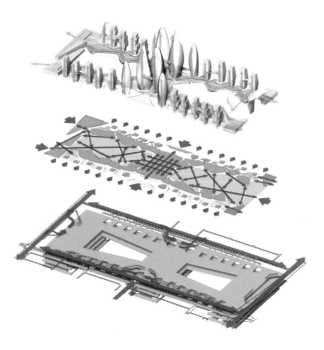

The overall plan of the complex shows the group of taller, rounded buildings at the center with the more linear and smaller towers at either end of the site, with substantial green spaces in between.

Die Gesamtansicht zeigt die Gruppe der höheren, abgerundeten Gebäude im Zentrum und die beidseitig davon aufgereihten niedrigeren und eckigeren Türme. Dazwischen liegen großzügige Grünanlagen.

Le plan d'ensemble du complexe montre le groupe d'immeubles arrondis de grande hauteur au centre, et les tours plus rectilignes et moins élevées aux deux extrémités du site, séparées par d'importants espaces verts.

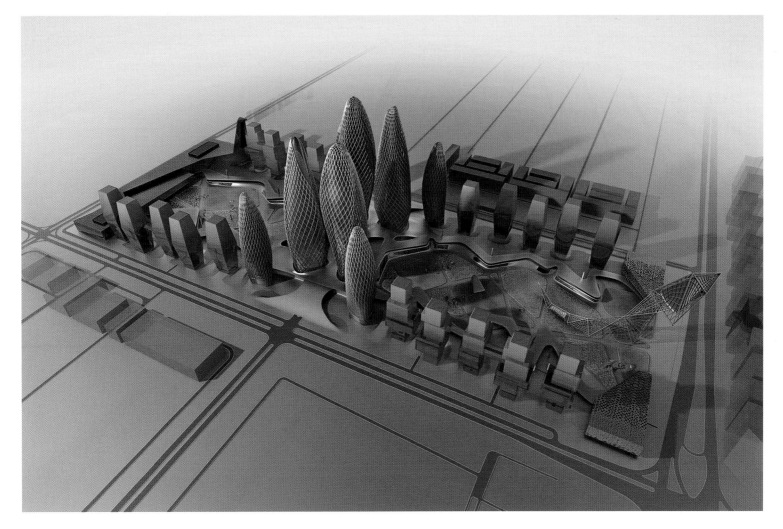

15

CARLOS OTT

CARLOS OTT ARCHITECT
Zonamerica
Business & Technology Park
Ruta 8 Km 17.5
Miniwarehouses – Off 216 – Atribar SA
CP 91 600
Montevideo, Uruguay

Tel: +598 2 518 2235
Fax: +598 2 518 2234
e-mail: montevideo@carlosott.com
Web: www.carlosott.com

CARLOS OTT was born in Montevideo in 1946. He received his first degree in Architecture from the University of Uruguay in Montevideo (1971), and M.Arch degrees from the Washington University School of Architecture (St. Louis, Missouri) and Hawaii University (Honolulu) in 1972. His completed projects include the Opera Bastille, Paris, France (1989); National Bank of Dubai, Dubai (1998, published here); Dubai Hilton Hotel, Dubai (2001); National Bank of Abu Dhabi, Abu Dhabi (2003, published here); Etisalat Headquarters, Abu Dhabi (2003), all in the UAE; and the Hangzhou Grand Theatre, Zhejiang, China (2004). He is working on the Dongguan Grand Theater, Guangdong, China; Calgary Federal Courthouse, Calgary, Canada; Ottawa Federal Court House, Ottawa, Canada; and the Henan Art Center, Zhenzhou, China. Carlos Ott became an international figure when he won the open, anonymous international competition for the Opera Bastille in Paris. His consistent and active presence in the UAE has made him one of the best-represented architects working there. Ott created his current firm in 1992 with a head office in Montevideo, Uruguay, and branches in Shanghai, Abu Dhabi, Toronto, Paris, and Montreal. In January 2006, the firm was employing 60 architects. Some of the other current work of Carlos Ott includes: Jade Beach I, a 55-story residential condominium under construction on a site facing the Atlantic Ocean in the Miami area; Artech, a 300-meter-long 10-story-high condominium facing the Intracoastal Waterway in the Miami area; Shenton Way #1, two towers including more than 360 residential units in Singapore; Regent Hotel and Residential Tower, a serviced apartment tower linked to the Regent Hotel in Kuala Lumpur, Malaysia; Infinity Towers, a 50-story residential complex in Guadalajara, Mexico; and the Hangzhou International Conference Center, a 400-room five-star hotel and conference and banquet hall, in Hangzhou, China.

NATIONAL BANK OF ABU DHABI
ABU DHABI, UAE
1997-2000

PARTNERS IN CHARGE: Carlos Ott, Adel Almojil
FLOOR AREA: 35 000 m^2
CLIENT: The National Bank of Abu Dhabi
COST: $107 million (1998 value)

Ott was the winner of an international competition for the design of this 33-story building (1995). He used a pyramidal cross section with "inversely reflected triangular peaks" in the design. The building is clad in gray glass and has a four-story transparent glass atrium in the entrance. The use of the gray glass, defined on the surface of the building by narrow bands corresponding to the floor levels, confers the type of image of solidity and discretion requested by the client. Lifted high above the ground on a slender column near the street corner, the building continues to stand out on the Abu Dhabi skyline. A large, inverted triangular volume clad in stone panels is suspended above the entrance area, contributing to the daring impression given by the architecture both from a distance and at close quarters. The use of such strong, geometric language in this context no longer appears to obey the contextual emphasis placed on the façade of the earlier National Bank of Dubai, yet it shares with the first structure a taste for suspended, essentially geometric volumes that add movement, and perhaps even a hint of daring, to these solid bank headquarters buildings.

1995 gewann Carlos Ott den internationalen Wettbewerb für die Nationalbank von Abu Dhabi. Die Form des 33-geschossigen Gebäudes beruht auf zwei Prismen mit »entgegengesetzt geneigten dreieckigen Spitzen«. Ein viergeschossiges transparentes Glasatrium bildet den Eingangsbereich des mit grau getöntem Glas verkleideten Baukörpers. Die Glasfassade wird durch schmale, geschossweise angeordnete Bänder strukturiert und vermittelt den vom Bauherrn gewünschten Eindruck von Solidität und Diskretion. Der Hauptbaukörper ist hoch über den Boden angehoben und ruht auf einer schlanken Stütze in der Nähe der Straßenecke. Dem Gebäude gelingt es, sich in Abu Dhabis Skyline zu behaupten. Ein überdimensionales, auf der Spitze stehendes und mit Naturstein verkleidetes Dreieck schwebt über dem Eingangsbereich und verstärkt den gewagten Eindruck, den die Architektur aus der Ferne und auch aus der Nähe macht. Im Gegensatz zur etwas früher fertiggestellten Nationalbank von Dubai scheint die klare geometrische Sprache nicht mehr auf einem kontextuellen Ansatz zu beruhen. Beides sind jedoch auskragende klare geometrische Baukörper, die den gediegenen Bankzentralen ein Moment der Bewegung, vielleicht sogar Kühnheit verleihen.

Ott avait cette fois encore remporté le concours international organisé pour la conception de cet immeuble de 33 niveaux (1995). Il a imaginé une pyramide déconstruite à « sommets inversés ». L'immeuble est habillé de verre gris, et doté à son entrée d'un atrium de verre transparent sur quatre niveaux de haut. Le verre gris, pris entre de fins bandeaux qui soulignent les niveaux, confère à ce siège l'image de solidité et de discrétion que recherchait le client. Surélevé par rapport au sol sur de minces colonnes à l'angle de la rue, l'immeuble se détache du panorama de la ville. Un important volume triangulaire habillé de panneaux de pierre, suspendu au-dessus de la zone d'entrée, contribue à ce sentiment de performance architecturale perceptible aussi bien de loin que de près. Le recours à un langage géométrique fort dans ce contexte ne reprend pas l'emphase contextuelle de la façade du précédent siège de la Banque Nationale de Dubaï, mais partage avec celui-ci un goût pour les volumes suspendus qui confèrent à ces massifs sièges de banque une impression de mouvement, et peut-être même d'audace.

The bank buildings by Carlos Ott in the region represent some of the earliest efforts on the part of the Emirates to call on talented architects rather than exclusively privilege large "corporate" architectural firms.

Carlos Otts Bankgebäude in der Golfregion gehen auf frühe Bemühungen der Emirate zurück, Aufträge an talentierte Architekten zu vergeben, anstatt ausschließlich große kommerzielle Architekturbüros zu berücksichtigen.

Les immeubles bancaires réalisés par Carlos Ott dans la région font partie des premières tentatives des Émirats de faire appel à des architectes de talent plutôt qu'à de grandes agences dites « institutionnelles ».

NATIONAL BANK OF DUBAI
DUBAI, UAE
1996-98

PARTNERS IN CHARGE: Carlos Ott, NORR
AREA: 40 000 m²
CLIENT: National Bank of Dubai
COST: $53 million (2000 value)

Carlos Ott was again the winner of an international design competition for this 124-meter-high tower located on the northeast side of Dubai Creek. As he explained its iconic design, "The headquarters of the National Bank of Dubai is based on the imagery of the dhow, a centuries-old regional boat used in the Indian Ocean, and the establishment of Dubai as a market place. Its curved curtain wall represents the billowing sail, supported by two granite columns. The base of the building, the banking hall, is clad in green glass representing the water and its roof of aluminum, the hull of the boat. The curved façade gives a reflection of the air and the Dubai Creek, although the most impressive show is at sundown when the unique sunsets allow for shades of gold and silver to shine off the curved mirror." Though it was completed before any other project in this book, the building retains a modernity that can best be attributed to its simple, surprising form, which does indeed change colors with the movement of the sun. Various architects have sought to give their buildings a feeling of local tradition, but Ott's has searched for an essence rather than any impractical quotation from desert buildings. Although Dubai has now entered a phase of extremely rapid construction of ever-higher towers, the National Bank of Dubai by Carlos Ott retains a symbolic presence in the city, as one of the first and most successful examples of deliberately iconic work done by a significant architect in the Emirate.

Das 124 m hohe Hochhaus befindet sich auf der nordöstlichen Seite des Dubai Creek. Carlos Ott, Gewinner des internationalen Wettbewerbs für die Zentrale, erläutert die zeichenhafte Form des Gebäudes: »Der Entwurf basiert auf dem Bild der Dau, dem traditionellen Boot, das seit Jahrhunderten auf dem Indischen Ozean fährt. Der Bank ging es darum, Dubai als Markt zu etablieren. Die geschwungene Vorhangfassade symbolisiert ein geblähtes Segel, das von zwei Granitstützen getragen wird. Der Sockel des Gebäudes mit der Schalterhalle ist in grünes Glas gekleidet und repräsentiert das Wasser; das Aluminiumdach der Halle erinnert an einen Schiffsrumpf. In der gewölbten Fassade spiegeln sich der Himmel und der Dubai Creek. Am beeindruckendsten ist die Fassade jedoch in der Abenddämmerung, wenn der gewölbte Spiegel während der einzigartigen Sonnenuntergänge golden und silbern schimmert.« Die Nationalbank von Dubai wurde früher als die anderen in diesem Buch vorgestellten Projekte gebaut, dennoch wirkt sie nach wie vor sehr modern. Dies ist auf ihre einfache, ungewöhnliche Form zurückzuführen, die mit dem Gang der Sonne ihre Farbe verändert. Verschiedene Architekten haben versucht, mit ihren Gebäuden regionale Bautraditionen zu interpretieren, Ott jedoch hat nach einer »Essenz« gesucht, statt irgendein Element eines traditionellen Wüstengebäudes bloß zu zitieren. Obwohl Dubai in eine Phase schwindelerregender Bautätigkeit eingetreten ist, in der immer höhere Wolkenkratzer in den Himmel wachsen, behält das Gebäude der Nationalbank von Dubai von Carlos Ott seine Präsenz in der Stadt. Es ist eines der ersten und erfolgreichsten Beispiele eines bewusst zeichenhaften Gebäudes, das von einem renommierten Architekten in Dubai entworfen wurde.

Cette tour de 124 m de haut, qui se dresse sur la côte nord-est de la crique de Dubaï, a fait l'objet d'un concours international remporté par Carlos Ott qui explique ainsi ce projet iconique : « Le siège de la Banque nationale de Dubaï repose sur l'iconographie du « dhow », un bateau local de forme très ancienne utilisé dans l'océan Indien, et sur la transformation de Dubaï en place financière. Son mur-rideau incurvé représente une voile gonflée, soutenue par deux colonnes de granit. La base – la salle de la banque – est habillée de verre de couleur verte qui représente l'eau, tandis que son toit en aluminium symbolise la proue du bateau. La façade incurvée prend les reflets du ciel et de la crique de Dubaï. Le moment le plus impressionnant se produit au coucher du soleil, lorsque ce miroir incurvé étincelle de nuances d'or et d'argent. » Achevé avant les autres projets présentés dans cet ouvrage, l'immeuble conserve une modernité que l'on peut attribuer à sa forme simple, et néanmoins surprenante, dont la couleur change selon les mouvements du soleil. Plusieurs architectes ont tenté d'utiliser des éléments tirés des traditions locales, mais Ott en a recherché l'essence plutôt que d'en faire une simple citation. Bien que Dubaï soit maintenant entrée dans une phase de construction extrêmement rapide de tours de plus en plus hautes, la Banque nationale maintient sa présence symbolique. Elle est un des premiers exemples, et le plus réussi, d'œuvre volontairement iconique réalisée par un architecte important dans l'émirat.

Lifted off the ground and contrasting its concrete support pillars with its glass-clad heart, the building is identifiable from a distance in the older, more traditional district of Dubai.

Die beiden Betonpfeiler kontrastieren mit dem zwischen ihnen schwebenden gläsernen Mittelteil. Der Bau in Dubais älterem, traditionellem Stadtteil ist auch aus der Entfernung leicht zu erkennen.

Surélevé par rapport au sol, opposant ses épais piliers de béton à une partie centrale intégralement vitrée, l'immeuble se repère de loin dans ce quartier plus ancien et plus traditionnel de Dubaï.

With its curving reflective surface and location near the water, the bank building remains an iconic presence in Dubai, located at some distance from the main new development zones such as Business Bay.

Die gewölbte, reflektierende Fassade und die Lage am Wasser sorgen für die zeichenhafte Präsenz des Bankgebäudes. Es befindet sich in einiger Entfernung zu den großen Stadtentwicklungsgebieten in Dubai, etwa der Business Bay.

Par ses surfaces incurvées réfléchissantes et sa situation en bord de mer, non loin des nouvelles zones de développement urbain comme la Business Bay, l'immeuble de la banque affirme sa présence iconique à Dubaï.

16

I. M. PEI

I. M. PEI, ARCHITECT
88 Pine Street
New York, NY 10 005
United States

Tel: +1 212 872 4010
Fax: +1 212 872 4222

Born in 1917 in Canton (now Guangzhou), China, **I. M. PEI** came to the United States in 1935. He received his B.Arch degree from MIT (1940); his M.Arch from Harvard (1942), and a doctorate from Harvard (1946). He formed I. M. Pei & Associates in 1955. He won the AIA Gold Medal (1979); the Pritzker Prize (1983); and the Praemium Imperiale in Japan (1989). His notable buildings include: the National Center for Atmospheric Research, Boulder, Colorado (1961-67); the Federal Aviation Agency Air Traffic Control Towers, 50 buildings, various locations (1962-70); the John F. Kennedy Library, Boston, Massachusetts (1965-79); the National Gallery of Art, East Building, Washington, D. C. (1968-78); the Bank of China Tower, Hong Kong (1982-89); the Grand Louvre, Paris, France (1983-93); the Rock and Roll Hall of Fame, Cleveland, Ohio (1993-95); and the Miho Museum, Shigaraki, Shiga, Japan (1992-97). He collaborated with his sons (Pei Partnership) on the recent Bank of China Headquarters, Beijing, China (1999-2001). His most recent projects include the German Historical Museum (Extension / Wechselausstellungsgebäude), Berlin, Germany; Mudam, Musée d'Art Moderne Grand-Duc Jean, Luxembourg; and the Suzhou Art Museum, Suzhou, China, inaugurated in 2006. His Museum of Islamic Art, Doha, Qatar (published here), is due for inauguration in late 2007.

MUSEUM OF ISLAMIC ART
DOHA, QATAR
2003 - 07

AREA: 35 000 m²
CLIENT: Qatar Museums Authority
COST: not disclosed
PROJECT TEAM: Perry Chin, Chris Rand,
Aslihan Demirtas, Hiroshi Okamoto
INTERIOR DESIGN: Jean-Michel Wilmotte

Located on an artificial island set 60 meters from the southern end of the prestigious Corniche in Doha, the new Museum of Islamic Art, due for inauguration late in 2007, is an ambitious project based in part in its design on I. M. Pei's search for the "essence" of Islamic architecture. Working on this design initially at the invitation of Luis Monreal, General Manager of the Aga Khan Trust for Culture, Pei found that the most pure expression of Islamic architecture was to be found in the Mosque of Ahmad Ibn Tulun (876–879), one of the oldest and purest of Cairo's monuments. Pei has developed a geometric progression "from the circle to the square and from the square to the octagon" based on his observation of Islamic designs. The spectacular entrance area of the museum, with its sweeping double staircase and 65-meter-high dome with a central oculus, is one of his finest and most sophisticated spaces. The actual exhibition spaces were designed by Jean-Michel Wilmotte of Paris, who has worked extensively with Pei in the past on such projects as the temporary exhibition areas under the Louvre Pyramid (1989) and the later Decorative Arts galleries in the same museum. In good part blank, without visible glazing on the land side, the Museum features an enormous opening on the side of the sea. A very large area of the new structure is devoted to teaching spaces, a library, and other facilities destined to bring Qatar up to international standards in the area of the study and appreciation of art. Pei's successful attempt to assimilate the lessons of his own knowledge of Western, modern architecture with those of the geometric Islamic traditions marks one of his most significant buildings outside of Western Europe and the United States.

Das Museum für islamische Kunst befindet sich auf einer künstlichen Insel, die in 60 m Entfernung vom südlichen Ende von Dohas prestigeträchtiger Corniche aufgeschüttet wurde. Ende 2007 soll der ehrgeizige Museumsbau eingeweiht werden. Entscheidend für den Entwurf war Peis Suche nach der Essenz islamischer Architektur. Pei, der ursprünglich von Luis Monreal, dem Geschäftsführer des Aga Khan Trust for Culture, gebeten worden war, das Museum zu entwerfen, stellte während der Arbeit am Entwurf fest, dass die 876 bis 879 errichtete Moschee von Ahmad Ibn Tulun, eines der ältesten und architektonisch reinsten Baudenkmäler von Kairo, das Wesen islamischer Architektur am klarsten zum Ausdruck bringt. Auf der Grundlage seiner Beschäftigung mit islamischer Baukunst schuf Pei eine geometrische Form, die sich »vom Kreis zum Quadrat und vom Quadrat zum Oktogon« entwickelt. Der spektakuläre Eingangsbereich des Museums mit seiner emporschwingenden Doppeltreppe und der 65 m hohen Kuppel mit dem zentralen Okulus ist einer der schönsten und anspruchsvollsten Räume, die Pei geschaffen hat. Die eigentlichen Ausstellungsräume wurden von Jean-Michel Wilmotte aus Paris gestaltet. Wilmotte hat bereits früher intensiv mit Pei zusammengearbeitet, etwa bei den Räumen für temporäre Ausstellungen unter der Louvre-Pyramide (1989) und später, ebenfalls im Louvre, bei den Räumen für Kunsthandwerk. Zum Land zeigt sich das Museum größtenteils geschlossen. Verglaste Flächen sind auf dieser Seite nicht sichtbar, zur Seeseite gibt es dagegen eine großflächige Öffnung. Einen großen Teil des Museums nehmen Unterrichtsräume, eine Bibliothek und andere Einrichtungen ein, die Katar bei der Auseinandersetzung mit und der Beurteilung von Kunst auf internationales Niveau bringen sollen. Peis erfolgreicher Versuch, sein Wissen über westliche moderne Architektur mit den tradierten geometrischen Formen der islamischen Kultur zu verknüpfen, charakterisiert eines seiner bedeutendsten Gebäude außerhalb Westeuropas und den USA.

Situé sur une île artificielle à 60 m de l'extrémité sud de la prestigieuse Corniche de Doha, le nouveau Musée d'art islamique, qui doit être inauguré fin 2007, est un ambitieux projet inspiré en partie des recherches de I. M. Pei sur l'essence de l'architecture islamique. Appelé initialement à travailler sur ce projet à l'invitation de Luis Monreal, directeur général de la Fondation Aga Khan pour la culture, Pei pense que l'expression la plus intense de l'architecture islamique se trouve dans la mosquée d'Ahmad Ibn Touloun (876–879), l'un des plus anciens et plus purs monuments du Caire. Il a ainsi mis au point une progression géométrique « du cercle au carré et du carré à l'octogone » d'après ses observations faites sur les réalisations islamiques. La spectaculaire zone d'entrée du musée à double escalier enveloppant et coupole à oculus central culminant à 65 m, est l'une de ses créations les plus belles et les plus sophistiquées. Les espaces d'expositions ont été conçus par Jean-Michel Wilmotte, qui avait déjà beaucoup travaillé avec Pei sur des projets comme les salles d'expositions temporaires de la Pyramide du Louvre (1989) et les galeries des arts décoratifs de ce même musée. En grande partie aveugle, sans ouvertures vitrées visibles du côté de la terre, le musée comporte en revanche une énorme baie du côté de la mer. Une zone très importante est consacrée à l'enseignement, à une bibliothèque et à des installations destinées à amener le Qatar au niveau des standards internationaux dans les domaines de l'étude et de l'appréciation de l'art. La tentative réussie de Pei, reposant sur son assimilation des leçons de sa connaissance de l'architecture occidentale moderne et de celles des traditions géométriques islamiques, fait de ce musée l'une de ses réalisations les plus significatives hors des États-Unis et de l'Europe.

Above, the museum seen on its artificially created site at the end of the Corniche. Below, plans show the large space devoted to an education wing (right on the plans).

Oben: das Museum an seinem künstlich angelegten Standort am Ende der Corniche; unten: Die Grundrisse zeigen die großen Flächen des Ausbildungstrakts (zu sehen rechts in den Grundrissen).

Ci-dessus, le musée sur son site artificiel à l'extrémité de la Corniche. Ci-dessous, les plans montrent le vaste volume consacré à l'éducation (à droite).

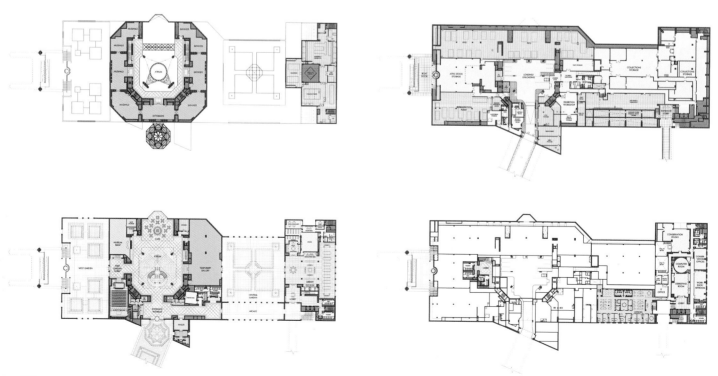

158

A circular basin and gardens have been created on one side of the museum. Below, an image taken from the water with the tall atrium-like window, one of the few actual openings that allow views from the inside to the exterior.

Auf einer Seite des Museums wurden ein rundes Meeresbassin und Gärten angelegt; unten: Blick vom Meer auf das hohe Fenster – eine der wenigen Öffnungen, die einen Ausblick nach draußen gewähren.

Un bassin circulaire et des jardins ont été créés sur un des côtés du musée. Ci-dessous, une image prise de la mer vers la grande baie de l'atrium, une des rares ouvertures qui autorisent des perspectives vers l'extérieur.

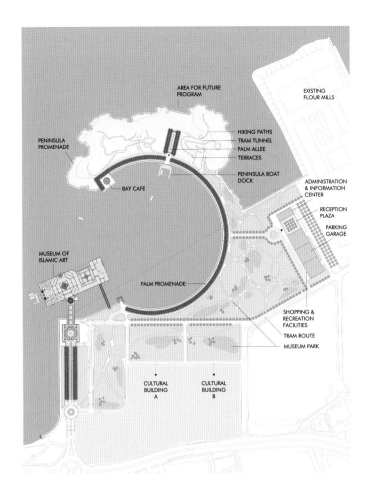

17

RNL

RNL DESIGN
800 Wilshire Blvd.
Suite 400
Los Angeles, California 90017
United States

Tel: +1 213 955 9775
Fax: +1 213 955 9885
e-mail: losangeles@rnldesign.com
Web: www.rnldesign.com

RNL is an international architecture, interiors, planning and engineering firm founded in 1956 with offices in Denver, Los Angeles and Phoenix, and affiliate offices in Dubai, UAE. RNL has worked with public and private clients in nearly 40 countries, including the United Arab Emirates, China, Egypt, Singapore, and Malaysia. Some of their most noteworthy projects are the master plan of Burj Dubai in the United Arab Emirates, and the Kuala Lumpur City Center development in Kuala Lumpur, Malaysia. RNL's other significant current projects include Sentosa Cove, Singapore (master planning); Najimat, Abu Dhabi (master planning); Wuxi, China (master planning); Union Park, Las Vegas (master planning with vertical architecture for some specific projects within the plan); Dubai Promenade (master planning and concept architecture design); and Lowry Range, Aurora, Colorado (master planning). Amongst the participants in the Shams Abu Dhabi project published here, David Klages received his B.Arch degree from the University of Southern California. He has worked as an architect and planner for over 40 years. He has worked in particular on a large number of golf club projects in California and Nevada. Patrick McKelvey received his B.Arch degree from the University of Michigan (1979) and his M.Arch from the same institution in 1981. A Principal and member of RNL's board, McKelvey joined the firm in 1987 and is responsible for the international practice. Cindy Teale is an Associate Principal of RNL and a design architect with considerable experience in the UAE. She has worked on the Shams Abu Dhabi project, and also on the Nakheel Jumeirah Pointe Villas, Dubai, UAE; the Burj Dubai master plan.

SHAMS ABU DHABI
ABU DHABI, UAE
2006 -

FLOOR AREA: 156 ha
CLIENT: Sorouh Real Estate Investments
COST: not disclosed
PROJECT TEAM: David Klages, Pat McKelvey,
Cindy Teale, Pat Dawe, Sai Balikrishnan,
Marc Stutzman, Amera Al-Awahi, James Leggitt

Reem Island is directly adjacent to the city of Abu Dhabi, on an island located in the Arabian Gulf approximately 200 meters from the mainland. Because of its proximity, the project will be seen as an extension of Abu Dhabi, but will "have its own distinct character" according to the architects. The 156-hectare site covers one-third of Reem Island. The architects explain that "the client brief was to plan a landmark new town development that would be an 'icon' of Abu Dhabi, providing a wonderful urban environment within which to live, work, be entertained, enjoy recreation areas, etc." A major loop roadway and access bridge from Abu Dhabi are significant elements in the project organization. A number of neighborhoods with their own character and identity are included in the master plan. "There are residential neighborhoods, both high-rise and low-rise; commercial office buildings, retail commercial areas, an entertainment district, urban hotels and a resort hotel, small marinas, and pedestrian promenades linking all of these elements." A major "iconic" building is to be located near the Central Park area of the project. This structure is envisaged as "a quad tower with the 80-story elements on each corner of the loop road, linked at the top by a domed structure." Energy and conservation issues have been carefully addressed in the project. The conservation of an existing mangrove area on the island is one priority, but, above all, the plan encourages the construction of "green" or sustainable designs.

Das Entwicklungsgebiet Reem liegt direkt neben Abu-Dhabi-Stadt auf der gleichnamigen, ca. 200 m vom Festland entfernten Insel im Golf. Aufgrund seiner Nähe zu Abu Dhabi wird das Gebiet als Stadterweiterung betrachtet, soll aber »einen eigenständigen Charakter haben«. Das 156 ha große Grundstück nimmt ein Drittel der Insel ein. Die Architekten erläutern: »Entsprechend den Vorgaben des Bauherrn sollte ein neues Stadtgebiet mit Wahrzeichencharakter geplant werden. Hier soll eine qualitätvolle städtische Umgebung entstehen, in der man wohnen und arbeiten kann und es Angebote zur Unterhaltung und Erholung usw. gibt.« Eine schlaufenförmige Hauptstraße und eine Brücke, die die Insel mit Abu Dhabi verbindet, sind wesentliche Elemente der Organisation des neuen Stadtteils. Der Masterplan sieht verschiedene Bereiche, jeweils mit eigener Identität, vor: »Es gibt Wohngebiete in Form von Hochhäusern oder als flache Bebauung, Bürohäuser, Einkaufsgebiete, ein Unterhaltungsviertel, städtische Hotels und ein Ferienhotel, kleine Marinas und Fußgängerpromenaden, die alle Bereiche miteinander verbinden.« Ein großes markantes Gebäude soll am zentral gelegenen Park entstehen. Es steht an der schlaufenförmigen Hauptstraße und besteht »aus einer Gruppe von vier 80-geschossigen Türmen, die durch eine gemeinsame Kuppel miteinander verbunden sind«. Energetische Aspekte und der Schutz der Natur werden bei diesem Projekt sorgfältig beachtet. Die Erhaltung eines Mangrovengebietes auf der Insel ist ein wichtiger Punkt, v. a. aber unterstützt der Masterplan den Bau »grüner« bzw. nachhaltiger Architektur.

L'île de Reem se trouve à 200 m environ de la côte, face à Abu Dhabi. Du fait de cette proximité, le projet est en fait une extension de la ville, mais possédera néanmoins « son propre caractère », selon les architectes. Le terrain de 156 hectares recouvre un tiers de l'île. Selon le descriptif de l'agence : « La demande du client était de créer une nouvelle zone urbaine monumentale, une « icône » d'Abu Dhabi, un environnement urbain merveilleux où l'on puisse vivre, travailler, se distraire, profiter de ses loisirs, etc. » Une route en boucle et un pont reliant le projet à Abu Dhabi font partie des composants majeurs de l'organisation urbanistique du projet. Plusieurs quartiers possédant chacun son caractère propre et son identité sont prévus dans le plan directeur. « Ce sont des quartiers résidentiels d'immeubles de grande hauteur ou non, d'immeubles de bureaux, d'équipements commerciaux de détail, avec un quartier pour sortir, des hôtels classiques et un hôtel de vacances, de petites marinas et des promenades piétonnières qui relient tous ces éléments. » Un immeuble majeur, lui aussi « iconique », devait s'élever près du parc central prévu. « Ce devrait être une quadruple tour, dont les quatre éléments de 80 niveaux se trouveraient en bordure d'une voie circulaire, reliés au sommet par une structure en coupole. » Les enjeux énergétiques et écologiques ont été soigneusement pris en compte. La conservation d'une mangrove existante est l'une des priorités, mais surtout, le plan encourage la construction de projets « verts ».

With projects such as this one and the Saadiyat Island
complex, Abu Dhabi is racing to catch up with Dubai in
terms of the sheer scale and ambition of its new urban
projects.

Abu Dhabi bemüht sich mit Dubai gleichzuziehen, z. B. mit
großen und ehrgeizigen Stadtplanungsprojekten wie diesem
oder der Insel Saadiyat.

Avec des projets comme celui-ci et le complexe de l'île de
Saadiyat, Abu Dhabi entre en compétition avec Dubaï sur
l'échelle extravagante et les ambitions de ses nouveaux
projets urbains.

18

HADI SIMAAN

HADI SIMAAN ARCHITECTS
3407 Kentshire Blvd.
Ocoee, Florida 34761
United States

Tel: +1 407 876 9899
Fax: +1 407 248 0071
e-mail: hadi@hadisimaan.com
Web: www.hadisimaan.com

HADI SIMAAN was born in Lebanon in 1958. He grew up in London and attended the Architectural Association (AA) beginning in 1975 at a time when Rem Koolhaas, Zaha Hadid, Bernard Tschumi, and Daniel Libeskind were teaching there. He worked with YRM Architects and Planners in London as a Senior Designer from 1985 to 1990, with Harasani Associates (London, 1990–99), and then at Farmer Baker Barrios and VOA in Orlando, Florida, before creating his own firm in Florida in 2001. Projects he has worked on since creating his own firm include: Grand National Towers, Orlando, Florida; a 660-meter mixed-use tower project for the UAE; Magnolia Tower, Orlando, Florida; Platinum Towers, Orlando, Florida; 1000 apartments building, Al Falah Bank, Abu Dhabi, UAE; the Sports City Tower, Doha, Qatar (published here); West Bay Hotel, Doha, Qatar; a $230-million mixed-use stadium, hotel, office, retail complex, Doha, Qatar; the BU2 Tower, Doha, Qatar (published here); City Center Hotel, Doha, Qatar; Hard Rock Café Headquarters, Orlando, Florida; and early work on the master plan for the Ringling Museum, Sarasota, Florida.

ASPIRE SPORTS CITY TOWER DOHA, QATAR 2004-07

DESIGN ARCHITECT: Hadi Simaan
PARTNERS IN CHARGE: Etienne Tricaud/AREP. John Hirst
AREA: 34 000 m²
CLIENT: Sheikh Jassim Bin Hamad al-Thani
COST: $187 million

At 300 meters, the Aspire Tower is presently the tallest structure in Qatar. It is located at the center of the Khalifa Sports City Complex in Doha. As the architect explains the genesis of the project, "I was invited by His Highness Sheikh Jassim Bin Hamad al-Thani to present a design for the Sports City landmark structure that was to house the flame for the 15th Asian games to be held in Doha between the 1st and the 15th of December 2006. His Highness was very specific in his vision for the project: a 300-meter-high landmark structure to be visibly identified as an Olympic flame. The size of the flame itself, and the height of its positioning, are both world records. Sheikh Jassim also requested that the structure house a five-star hotel with a spa and a revolving restaurant at the top." The hotel was not completed in time for the Games, but the Tower was. The wrapping stainless-steel façade encircling a structural concrete core encloses two levels of offices (2600 m²), a gymnasium, health club, sports museum, 80-person revolving restaurant, 200-person panoramic observation deck and bar (at a height of 240 m), and the hotel with about 137 rooms. At 215 meters, the revolving restaurant is the highest in the Middle East. A 170-place ballroom and banqueting suite, a conference-business center, and franchise space complete the program. A sky beam is to project from the tower's crown. The lobby features a 63-meter-high atrium. Hadi Simaan further explains that aside from the heart of the tower, "The remainder of the building is a steel structure that hangs and cantilevers out from the concrete core. I think this is also a first, to hang the building from the core." The engineer John Hirst from Arup participated actively in this structural solution. Simaan concludes, "The overall composition of the building as a sculpture creates an extremely energetic aesthetic with a rigor that enforces a sense of equilibrium. This sense of energy versus equilibrium plays back and forth in the mind of the spectator a bit like watching the flame of a campfire under the night sky."

Mit 300 m ist der Aspire Tower im Zentrum von Dohas Khalifa Sports City Complex derzeit das höchste Gebäude in Katar. Der Architekt beschreibt die Entstehung des Projekts: »Seine Hoheit Scheich Jassim Bin Hammed al-Thani lud mich ein, einen Entwurf für ein Wahrzeichen der Sports City zu erarbeiten, in dem die Flamme der in Doha vom 1. bis zum 15. Dezember 2006 stattfindenden 15. Asienspiele brennen sollte. Seine Hoheit hatte sehr genaue Vorstellungen von dem Projekt: Ein 300 m hohes Wahrzeichen, das als Olympische Flamme zu erkennen sein sollte. Sowohl die Größe der Flamme als auch die Höhe, in der sie brennt, sind Weltrekord. Scheich Jassim wünschte außerdem ein Fünf-Sterne-Hotel mit Spa sowie ein sich um die eigene Achse drehendes Restaurant an der Spitze des Turms.« Das Hotel konnte nicht bis zu den Spielen fertiggestellt werden, wohl aber der Turm. Eine Edelstahlfassade umhüllt den tragenden Betonkern sowie zwei Bürogeschosse (2600 m²), eine Sporthalle, einen Fitnessclub, ein Sportmuseum, das Restaurant für 80 Personen, eine Aussichtsplattform für 200 Personen mit Bar in 240 m Höhe und das Hotel mit 137 Zimmern. Auf 215 m Höhe ist das Restaurant das höch-

ste im Nahen Osten. Ein Ballsaal mit 170 Plätzen sowie ein Bankettsaal, ein Konferenz-Businesscenter und Franchiseräume ergänzen das Programm. Von der Spitze des Turms soll ein Laserstrahl (Sky Beam) ausgesendet werden. Die Höhe der Lobby beträgt 63 m. Hadi Simaan erläutert, dass abgesehen von dem Gebäudekern »der Rest des Gebäudes aus einer Stahlkonstruktion besteht, die am Gebäudekern abgehängt ist und von ihm auskragt. Ich glaube, es ist sehr wichtig, dass die Konstruktion am Kern hängt«. Der Ingenieur John Hirst vom Büro Arup hatte wesentlichen Einfluss auf die konstruktive Lösung. Simaan stellt fest: »Ein Gebäude als Skulptur – dieses Konzept schafft eine extrem dynamische Ästhetik mit einer Kraft, die das Gefühl eines Gleichgewichts verstärkt. Die gleichzeitige Wahrnehmung von Energie und Gleichgewicht geht im Kopf des Betrachters hin und her, als würde man ein Lagerfeuer unter einem Nachthimmel betrachten.«

Avec ses 300 m de haut, la tour Aspire représente actuellement le plus haut immeuble du Qatar. Elle se trouve au centre du complexe de la Khalifa Sports City à Doha. L'architecte explique ainsi la genèse de ce projet : « J'ai été invité par son Altesse le cheikh Jassim Bin Hammad al-Thani à proposer des plans pour un immeuble phare à construire dans le complexe de la « Cité des sports », qui devait accueillir la flamme des 15e Jeux asiatiques prévus à Doha, du 1er au 15 décembre 2006. Son Altesse avait une vision très précise du projet : une tour monumentale de 300 m de haut dont la forme évoquerait la flamme olympique. La taille de la flamme elle-même et la hauteur de son positionnement représentent des records mondiaux. Le cheikh Jassim a également demandé que l'immeuble comprenne un hôtel cinq étoiles, un spa et un restaurant tournant au sommet. » L'hôtel ne fut pas achevé pour les Jeux, mais la tour le fut. La façade enveloppante en acier inoxydable encerclant un noyau central en béton structurel recouvre deux étages de bureaux (2600 m²), un gymnase, un club de remise en forme, un musée du sport, un restaurant tournant de 80 couverts, un observatoire panoramique pour 200 personnes, un bar à 240 m d'altitude, et l'hôtel de 137 chambres. Le restaurant situé à 215 m d'altitude est le plus haut du Moyen-Orient. Une salle de bal et de banquet de 170 places, un centre d'affaires et de conférences et un espace de boutiques franchisées complètent ce programme. Un projecteur rayonne du sommet de l'édifice. Le hall d'accueil est en forme d'atrium de 63 m de haut. Hadi Simaan explique également que « le reste du bâtiment est une structure en acier suspendue et en porte-à-faux par rapport à ce noyau central. Je pense qu'il s'agit là aussi d'une première : suspendre un immeuble à partir de son noyau ». L'ingénieur John Hirst de l'agence Arup a participé activement à la mise au point de la solution structurelle. « La composition sculpturale de l'ensemble a suscité une esthétique extrêmement énergétique, mais dont la rigueur renforce l'impression d'équilibre. Ce sentiment d'énergie en opposition avec l'équilibre joue alternativement dans l'esprit du spectateur, un peu comme lorsqu'on observe un feu de camp sous un ciel nocturne. »

A view of the interior atrium space, and, right, an image showing the unusual exterior lighting design that heightens the building's presence after dark.

Blick in das Atrium; rechts: Das ungewöhnliche Beleuchtungskonzept verstärkt die Präsenz des Gebäudes in der Nacht.

Vue de l'atrium et, à droite, une vision du surprenant éclairage nocturne qui magnifie la présence élancée de l'immeuble.

Not visible from the center of Doha, the tower announced the sport city complex in an undeniably iconic way.

Vom Zentrum Dohas aus ist der Turm, Wahrzeichen des Sport City Complex, nicht zu sehen.

Non visible du centre de Doha, la tour annonce la présence de ce complexe sportif d'une manière indiscutablement axée sur l'image.

BUZWAIR TOWER (BU2) DOHA, QATAR 2006 -

AREA: 84 300 m^2
HEIGHT: 235 m
CLIENT: Saad Buzwair
COST: $130 million

This unusual tower is to be 235 meters high. The original site measured 175 meters deep for 225 meters of beach frontage, but this lot was sold and the project is awaiting a new site. Hadi Simaan explains, "The idea is to have the hotel on the lower floors and the apartments on the upper floors, with recreation and resort-type facilities in the base. I like it because it represents an iconic image. Sometimes these iconic and memorable designs are hard to achieve because they require a certain balance between complexity and simplicity. This project I think does that." The structure at the top of the tower is steel with steel-mesh cladding intended to house light shows. The diameter of the main tower is 61 meters. A stepped structure facing the beach contains the hotel "chalets" with private balconies, and a private penthouse villa is located at the very top. As he did for the Aspire Sports City Tower, the architect proposes a form that would be readily recognizable even in a city that is developing very rapidly with a large number of unusually shaped tall buildings. Hadi Simaan combines a Middle Eastern background with an English education and an American base, factors that will undoubtedly contribute to his continuing success in areas such as Qatar or the United Arab Emirates.

Einmal fertiggestellt, wird der ungewöhnliche Wolkenkratzer eine Höhe von 235 m erreichen. Das ursprünglich vorgesehene Grundstück direkt am Meer war 175 m tief und 225 m breit, es wurde jedoch verkauft, und so wartet der Entwurf auf ein neues Grundstück. Hadi Simaan erläutert: »Die Idee besteht darin, in den unteren Geschossen ein Hotel und in den oberen Geschossen Apartments vorzusehen; im Sockelbereich sind badeorttypische Einrichtungen sowie Freizeitanlagen angeordnet. Mir gefällt das Haus, weil es ein markantes Bild transportiert. Manchmal gelingen diese zeichenhaften und einprägsamen Entwürfe nur sehr schwer, weil sie eine Balance zwischen Komplexität und Einfachheit erfordern. Ich glaube, dieses Gebäude hält diese Balance.« Die Konstruktion der Gebäudespitze besteht aus Stahl und ist mit einer netzartigen Stahlverkleidung versehen, hinter der sich die Technik für Lichtshows verbirgt. Der Durchmesser des Turms beträgt 61 m. In den zum Strand abgestuften Geschossen befinden sich Hotel-Chalets mit eigenen Balkonen, den oberen Abschluss bildet jeweils eine Penthousevilla. Wie beim Aspire Sports City Tower schlägt der Architekt eine Form vor, die – auch in einer Stadt, die sich so rasant entwickelt wie Doha und die mit sehr vielen auffälligen Wolkenkratzern aufwartet – einen hohen Wiedererkennungswert hat. Hadi Simaan, der aus dem Nahen Osten stammt, wurde in Großbritannien ausgebildet, sein Büro befindet sich in Amerika. Diese Faktoren tragen sicherlich zu seinem beständigen Erfolg in Ländern wie Katar und den Vereinigten Arabischen Emiraten bei.

Cette tour étonnante devrait s'élever à 235 m de haut. Le terrain visé de 175 x 225 m en front de mer ayant été vendu, le projet est en attente d'une nouvelle opportunité foncière. Selon Hadi Simaan : « L'idée est de placer l'hôtel dans les niveaux inférieurs et les appartements en partie supérieure, des équipements de loisirs de type resort occupant le socle. J'aime beaucoup ce projet pour sa valeur iconique. Ce type d'entreprise à haute visibilité est parfois délicat car il faut trouver un certain équilibre entre la complexité et la simplicité. Je pense que cette tour réussit à l'atteindre. » La structure sommitale, d'où partiront des effets lumineux, est à enveloppe en treillis d'acier. Le diamètre de la tour principale est de 61 m. La structure en gradins face à la plage contient les « chalets » de l'hôtel dotés de balcons privatifs, et une villa en penthouse à son sommet. Comme pour la tour Aspire, l'architecte a proposé une forme facilement identifiable, dans une ville qui multiplie rapidement les immeubles de grande hauteur d'aspect inhabituel. Hadi Simaan associe une culture orientale à une éducation britannique et une formation américaine, facteurs qui contribuent certainement à son succès dans des pays comme le Qatar ou les Émirats arabes unis.

The lozenge-like forms of the tower give it an unexpected presence on the skyline, with its enormous arched opening at the top further calling attention to the project.

Seine überraschende, an ein Lutschbonbon erinnernde Form verleiht dem Gebäude seine Präsenz in der Skyline. Die große bogenförmige Öffnung an der Spitze des Turms sorgt zusätzlich für Aufmerksamkeit.

La forme en losange de la tour lui confère une personnalité particulière qui se détache dans le panorama urbain. L'énorme ouverture en arc du sommet attire les regards.

19

SKIDMORE, OWINGS & MERRILL

SKIDMORE, OWINGS & MERRILL LLP
224 South Michigan
Chicago, Illinois 60604
United States

Tel: +1 312 360 4973
Fax: +1 312 360 4554
e-mail: somchicago@som.com
Web: www.som.com

SKIDMORE, OWINGS AND MERRILL LLP (SOM) is one of the largest architecture firms in the United States. Founded in Chicago in 1936 by Louis Skidmore and Nathaniel Owings (John Merrill joined the firm in 1939), they have worked on some of the best-known skyscrapers in the US, including Lever House, New York (1952); John Hancock Center, Chicago (1969); and the Sears Tower, Chicago (1973). Some of the more famous partners of the firm have included Gordon Bunshaft, Bruce Graham, and more recently David Childs, who has taken over the Freedom Tower project from Daniel Libeskind on the Ground Zero site in lower Manhattan, and Adrian Smith, designer of the Burj Dubai Tower published here. Other recent work includes the 420-meter Jin Mao Tower in Pudong, Shanghai, China (1998); the Time Warner Center at Columbus Circle in New York (2003); and Terminal 3 at Ben Gurion Airport, Tel Aviv, Israel (in association with Moshe Safdie, 2004). Other current projects include the Pearl River Tower, Guangzhou, China; Trump International Hotel and Tower, Chicago; and Nanjing Greenland Financial Center, Nanjing, China. Adrian Smith, who studied architecture at the University of Chicago and was with SOM for 40 years, becoming a Partner in 1980, is also the designer of the Trump Hotel. He left SOM in October 2006 to create his own firm with Gordon Gill. Whatever the plans of Smith, the identity of SOM has long since evolved beyond the question of specific architects. It is the quintessential large, quality architectural firm that many have tried to imitate without great success.

BURJ DUBAI
DUBAI, UAE
2004 - 09

CLIENT: Emaar Properties PJSC, Dubai
HEIGHT: over 700 m
COST: not disclosed

Part of the appeal of the massive Burj Dubai Tower in Dubai was that it was billed from the outset as the tallest building in the world, and yet its exact height was made an absolute secret. Work started on the tower in January 2004. In March 2007, with 3000 workers on the site, the tower had reached a height of 380 meters and 110 levels, making it the tallest structure in the Middle East and Europe. "Burj Dubai is not a mere vertical conquest or a race for fame; it is an icon for the collective aspiration of the people of Dubai, who have been led to dream of the impossible and attain it," said Mr. Mohamed Ali Alabbar, Chairman of Emaar Properties. "Burj Dubai," according to Alabbar, "is an accomplishment of teamwork that involves some of the most brilliant minds in architecture, engineering, and construction." The tower is to include 1000 residences, commercial spaces, leisure facilities, and the Armani Hotel, Dubai, developed with Giorgio Armani, the Italian fashion designer. Burj Dubai is the centerpiece of the ($20 billion) Downtown Burj Dubai, "a mixed-use project in the heart of Dubai featuring residences, commercial space, hospitality projects, and several retail outlets, including the Dubai Mall, the world's largest shopping and entertainment destination." Adrian Smith, the designer of Burj Dubai, admits that he was thinking of the towers of the Emerald City in the film version of *The Wizard of Oz*. "That was in my mind as I was designing Burj Dubai," he said, "although in a subliminal way." "I didn't research the way it looked. I just remembered the glassy, crystalline structure coming up in the middle of what seemed like nowhere. The funny thing is, I didn't remember it being green." Emaar Properties originally wanted a tower of approximately 550 meters in height, but the designer persuaded them to go higher still. "At the very top, it didn't feel like it was resolved properly," Smith said. "I kept adding height, and got to a point where it could be a more continuous extrusion of elements of the building below it, instead of feeling like a base and a top with no middle," he says. According to the developers, the design of the building, made up of three elements grouped around the central core rising into a single spire, is derived from the form of local desert flowers. The thirst for height may not have been quenched in Dubai. As this book went to press plans for an even taller building were being laid.

Der Reiz des gewaltigen Burj Dubai liegt u. a. darin, dass er von Planungsbeginn an als das höchste Gebäude der Welt annonciert wurde, seine exakte Höhe jedoch streng geheim gehalten wird. Die Bauarbeiten begannen im Januar 2004. Im März 2007, als 3000 Arbeiter auf der Baustelle arbeiteten, hatte der Turm eine Höhe von 380 m bzw. 110 Geschossen erreicht. Damit ist er bereits das höchste Gebäude im Nahen Osten und Europa. »Im Burj Dubai manifestiert sich mehr als die symbolische Eroberung des Himmels oder der Wettstreit um Ruhm; er ist ein Symbol für das kollektive Streben der Menschen in Dubai, nicht nur vom Unmöglichen zu träumen, sondern es auch zu erreichen«, sagt Mohamed Ali Alabbar, Vorsitzender von Emaar Properties. Alabbar erläutert: »Burj Dubai ist das Resultat von Teamwork, an dem einige der brillantesten Köpfe beteiligt sind, die es in den Bereichen Architektur, Ingenieurwesen und Bauerrichtung derzeit gibt.« In dem Turm werden rund 1000 Wohnungen, Büros, Freizeiteinrichtungen und das Armani Hotel Dubai untergebracht sein. Das Hotel wird in Zusammenarbeit mit dem italienischen Modedesigner Giorgio Armani gestaltet. Der Burj Dubai ist das Herzstück des mit 20 Milliarden Dollar veranschlagten Stadtteils Downtown Burj Dubai im Zentrum Dubais, eines »Projekts mit Wohnungen, kommerziellen Flächen, gastronomischen Angeboten und mehreren Einkaufszentren, darunter die Dubai Mall, das weltgrößte Shopping- und Unterhaltungscenter.« Adrian Smith, Schöpfer des Burj Dubai, räumt ein, dass er an die Türme der Smaragdstadt aus dem Film »Der Zauberer von Oz« dachte: »Ich dachte an sie, als ich den Burj Dubai entwarf«, sagt er, »allerdings eher unbewusst. Ich habe nicht nachgeforscht, wie sie aussahen. Ich habe mich nur an die gläsernen, kristallinen Türme erinnert, die aus dem Nichts emporwuchsen. Das Lustige ist, ich hatte vergessen, dass sie grün waren.« Emaar Properties wollte ursprünglich ein rund 550 m hohes Gebäude, der Architekt überzeugte den Projektentwickler jedoch davon, noch höher zu bauen. »Ich hatte das Gefühl, dass die Gestaltung der Spitze nicht gut gelöst war«, sagt Smith. »Ich machte den Turm also immer höher und kam zu dem Punkt, wo er eher wie eine aus dem unteren Teil herausgezogene Form wirkte und nicht wie ein Gebäude mit einem Sockel und einer Spitze ohne etwas dazwischen«, sagt Smith. Laut Emaar Properties geht die Form des Turms auf die Form einer Wüstenblume zurück.

Une partie de l'intérêt porté à cette énorme Burj Dubaï tient à ce qu'elle a été annoncée, dès le départ, comme l'immeuble le plus haut du monde, même si sa hauteur reste un secret absolu. Les travaux ont débuté en janvier 2004. En mars 2007, 3000 ouvriers travaillaient sur le site et la tour avait déjà atteint 380 m pour 110 niveaux, déjà le plus haut immeuble du Moyen-Orient et d'Europe. « La Burj Dubaï n'est pas juste un record d'altitude ou une course à la gloire, c'est l'icône des aspirations collectives du peuple de Dubaï, qui a été conduit à rêver l'impossible et à l'atteindre », déclare Mohamed Ali Alabbar, président d'Emaar Properties. La Burj Dubaï est l'aboutissement d'un travail d'équipe qui a fait appel à quelques-uns des esprits les plus brillants du monde dans les domaines de l'architecture, de l'ingénierie et de la construction. » La tour contiendra 1000 appartements, des espaces commerciaux, des installations de loisirs et l'Armani Hotel, en collaboration avec le couturier italien. Burj Dubaï est l'élément central d'une opération urbanistique de 20 milliards de dollars, avec le Downtown Burj Dubaï, « projet polyvalent situé au cœur de Dubaï, comprenant des appartements, des espaces commerciaux, des équipements d'accueil, des magasins de détail, dont le Dubaï Mall, le plus grand centre commercial et de loisirs du monde ». Adrian Smith, son concepteur a admis qu'il avait pensé aux tours de la Cité d'émeraude de la version filmée du *Magicien d'Oz*. « Je l'avais en tête lorsque je dessinais la Burj Dubaï, bien que de façon subliminale... Je ne suis pas allé voir à quoi tout cela ressemblait. Je me souvenais seulement de constructions cristallines s'élevant au milieu de ce qui n'avait l'air de rien. La chose amusante est que je ne me rappellais pas la couleur verte. » Emaar Properties souhaitait au départ une tour d'environ 550 m de haut, mais l'architecte a réussi à les persuader d'aller encore plus loin. « Arrivé à l'extrême pointe du sommet, je n'avais pas l'impression d'avoir trouvé la bonne solution, dit-il, on n'arrêtait pas de monter. Cette tour se devait d'être davantage l'extrusion continue des éléments du bâtiment situés en dessous, plutôt que de donner l'impression d'avoir une base et un sommet sans rien entre les deux. » Selon les promoteurs, la conception de cette tour s'est inspirée de la forme de fleurs du désert local. La soif d'aller toujours plus haut n'a pas encore été étanchée à Dubaï. En effet, au moment de mettre sous presse ce livre, est annoncé un immeuble encore plus élevé ...

The Burj Dubai project stands in the midst of a very large development area, due to include residential and office space as well as one of the largest shopping malls in the world (entrance view below).

Der Burj Dubai befindet sich mitten in einem gigantischen Stadtentwicklungsgebiet mit Wohn- und Bürogebäuden sowie einer der weltweit größten Shopping-Malls; unten: der Eingang zur Mall.

Le projet de la Burj Dubaï s'élève au milieu d'une très vaste zone d'urbanisation qui comprendra des bureaux, des logements et l'un des plus grands centres commerciaux du monde (vue de l'entrée ci-dessous).

Though the exact height of the tower was a closely kept secret at the moment this book went to press, it is clear that it will remain the tallest building in the world for some time. Left, above, a construction view taken early in 2007.

Die exakte Höhe des Turms war bis zur Drucklegung ein streng gehütetes Geheimnis. Fest steht jedoch, dass er für eine Zeit lang das höchste Gebäude der Welt sein wird; links oben: die Baustelle Anfang 2007.

Bien que la hauteur exacte de la tour soit encore un secret bien gardé au moment de l'impression de ce livre, il est certain qu'elle sera un des immeubles les plus hauts du monde pour un certain temps. À gauche, page ci-contre, une vue du chantier prise début 2007.

20

VARIOUS ARCHITECTS
GUGGENHEIM PAVILIONS

Working in collaboration with the Solomon R. Guggenheim Foundation, the Tourism Development and Investment Company of Abu Dhabi (TDIC), called on Tadao Ando, Zaha Hadid, Frank Gehry, and Jean Nouvel to build museums in the Cultural District of Saadiyat Island, located just off the coast of Abu Dhabi. Part of the plan, developed in part by Guggenheim Foundation Director Thomas Krens, is to have approximately 19 pavilions to be used for the exhibition of art and in particular to house shows during the Abu Dhabi Biennale, meant eventually to rival that of Venice for contemporary art. Three of the designs for these pavilions, all to be located in the same vicinity as the museums, by Asymptote, Greg Lynn, and Pei-Zhu from Beijing are published here.

ASYMPTOTE ARCHITECTURE GROUP
160 Varick Street, Floor 10
New York, NY 10013
United States

Tel: +1 212 343 7333
Fax: +1 212 343 7099
e-mail: info@asymptote.net
Web: www.asymptote.net

GREG LYNN FORM
1817 Lincoln Blvd
Venice, California 90291
United States

Tel: +1 310 821 2629
Fax: +1 310 821 9729
e-mail: node@glform.com
Web: www.glform.com

STUDIO PEI-ZHU
B-413 Tianhai Business Center
No.107 N Dongsi Street
Beijing, 100007
China

Tel: +86 10 6401 6657
Fax: +86 10 6403 8967
e-mail: office@studiozp.com

ASYMPTOTE
ABU DHABI, UAE
2007-

FLOOR AREA: 5000 m² and 2500 m²
CLIENT: Tourism Development and Investment
Company of Abu Dhabi (TDIC),
Solomon R. Guggenheim Foundation
COST: not disclosed

Rather than designing just one pavilion, Hani Rashid and Lise Anne Couture chose to create two "enigmatic forms seemingly engaged in a profound and silent dialogue." As Rashid explains, "Asymptote's designs for the Guggenheim Pavilions on Saadiyat Island in Abu Dhabi are comprised of two elegantly sculpted vessels. These two articulated shells primarily house two 'big box' galleries for the exhibiting and viewing of contemporary art within a flexible and dynamic interior. The buildings are designed with state-of-the-art structural, enclosure and material technologies that in concert achieve a high performance building envelope and a powerful tectonic elegance of the highest order." The designs are described in part as being stone or "jewel-like." Light is filtered through the openings in the upper parts of the pavilions. A bridge designed by the firm would link the two structures across a canal on the site.

Anstelle eines einzelnen Pavillons schlagen Hani Rashid und Lise Anne Couture zwei »rätselhafte Formen vor, die, so scheint es, einen ernsten und stillen Dialog miteinander führen«. Rashid erläutert: »Asymptotes Entwurf für die Guggenheim-Pavillons auf Saadiyat besteht aus zwei elegant geformten ›Gefäßen‹. Die beiden beweglichen Gehäuse beherbergen vorrangig zwei ›Big-box‹-Galerien, in denen zeitgenössische Kunst in flexiblen und dynamischen Innenräumen präsentiert und betrachtet werden kann. Bei den Pavillons kommen die neuesten Konstruktions-, Fassaden- und Materialtechnologien zum Einsatz. Das Zusammenspiel der Technologien ermöglicht die Konstruktion der hocheffizienten Gebäudehüllen und eine kraftvolle tektonische Eleganz höchster Güte.« Daneben werden die beiden Gebäude auch als stein- oder juwelenartig beschrieben. Durch Öffnungen in den oberen Bereichen gelangt gefiltertes Licht in den Innenraum. Die auf beiden Seiten eines Kanals angeordneten Pavillons sind über eine ebenfalls von Asymptote entworfene Brücke miteinander verbunden.

Plutôt que de ne concevoir qu'un seul pavillon, Hani Rashid et Lise Anne Couture ont décidé de créer « deux formes énigmatiques qui paraissent engagées dans un dialogue profond et silencieux ». Selon la présentation de Rashid : « Les projets d'Asymptote pour les pavillons Guggenheim... se composent de deux vaisseaux élégamment sculptés. Ces deux coques articulées abritent essentiellement deux galeries, deux « grosses boîtes » pour l'exposition d'œuvres d'art contemporain dans un volume intérieur flexible et dynamique. Elles bénéficient de technologies structurelles et de matériaux d'avant-garde qui, ensemble, permettent d'obtenir une enveloppe performante et une élégance tectonique à la fois puissante et du plus haut niveau. » Les designs sont décrits comme des pierres ou des « joyaux ». La lumière est filtrée par des ouvertures en partie supérieure. Une passerelle, également conçue par l'agence, reliera les deux structures au-dessus d'un canal traversant le site.

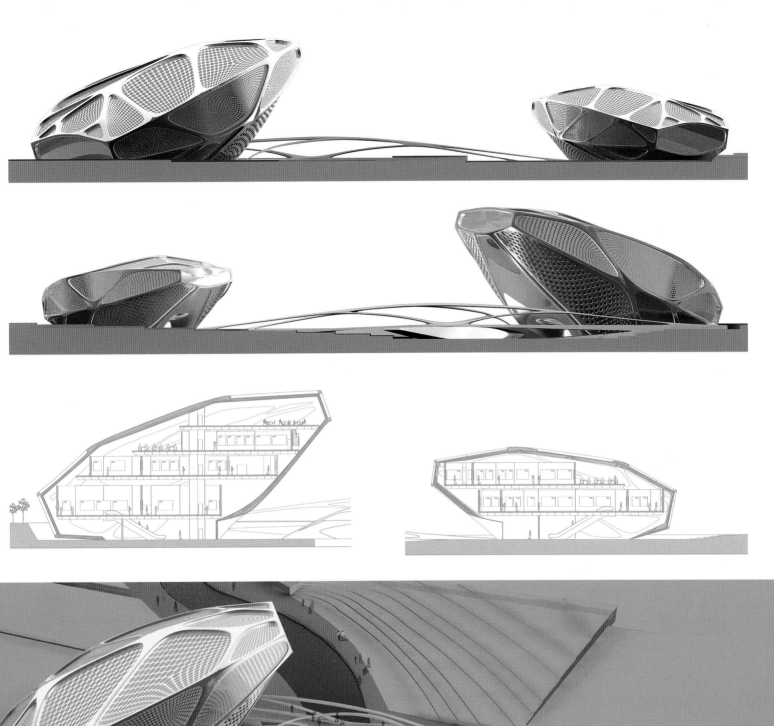

GREG LYNN FORM
ABU DHABI, UAE
2007-

FLOOR AREA: 5000 m²
CLIENT: Tourism Development and Investment
Company of Abu Dhabi (TDIC),
Solomon R. Guggenheim Foundation
COST: not disclosed
STRUCTURAL ENGINEER: Bruce Gibbons,
Thornton Tomasetti

Greg Lynn's plan for one gallery in the Saadiyat Island cultural complex is typically ambitious and surprising. A 100-meter-long exhibition space, café and bookshop is housed partially in a bridge over a river. Steel and glass structural tubes rise up from the bridge, becoming "lobby towers." A series of domed spaces on either side of the bridge evoke Muslim architecture. The actual six-meter-high gallery space, measuring a total of 3100 square meters, can be used as a single, continuous entity, or broken up into as many as 32 rooms as required. Developing on the sort of flower-like patterns seen in his design for the Ark of the World Museum (San Jose, Costa Rica, 2002), Greg Lynn gives a biological appearance to a structure that should be truly flexible in terms of the variety of exhibition possibilities it offers, while making a nod to the architecture of Islam as well.

Greg Lynns Entwurf für einen Ausstellungspavillon im Kulturdistrikt auf Saadiyat ist – wie üblich – ehrgeizig und überraschend. Ein 100 m langer Ausstellungsraum, ein Café und ein Buchladen werden überwiegend in einem Brückengebäude über einem Kanal untergebracht. Aus dieser Brücke wachsen röhrenartige Gebilde aus Stahl und Glas empor, die als Eingangstürme fungieren. Eine Abfolge von überkuppelten Räumen zu beiden Seiten der Brücke erinnert an muslimische Architektur. Der eigentliche, 6 m hohe Galerieraum mit einer Gesamtfläche von 3100 m² kann als Ganzes oder aber unterteilt in bis zu 32 Räume genutzt werden. Aufbauend auf seinem Entwurf für das Ark of the World Museum (San José, Costa Rica, 2002) entwickelt Lynn seine blumenartigen Muster weiter und gibt dem Pavillon ein biomorphes Aussehen. In Bezug auf die Ausstellungsmöglichkeiten ist das Gebäude tatsächlich sehr flexibel; ein wenig verneigt es sich auch vor der islamischen Architektur.

Les plans de Greg Lynn pour cette galerie du complexe culturel de l'île de Saadiyat est, à sa façon caractéristique, à la fois ambitieux et surprenant. Un volume de 100 m de long, un café et une librairie sont partiellement logés à l'intérieur d'un pont franchissant une rivière. Des tubes structurels en verre et acier qui s'élèvent de ce pont constituent les « tours du hall d'accueil ». De chaque côté de ce franchissement, une série d'espaces abrités sous des coupoles évoque l'architecture musulmane. La galerie elle-même, de 6 m de haut et de 3100 m² de surface, peut être utilisée comme telle, ou divisée en salles — jusqu'à 32 —, selon les besoins. Travaillant sur des motifs en fleurs déjà abordés pour son projet d'Ark of the World Museum (San Jose, Costa Rica, 2002), Greg Lynn donne un aspect biologique à ce bâtiment qui devrait offrir une grande souplesse en termes de possibilités d'expositions, tout en saluant au passage l'architecture islamique.

STUDIO PEI-ZHU
ABU DHABI, UAE
2007-

PARTNERS IN CHARGE: Mark Broom, Xiaoming Zeng
AREA: 3500 m²
CLIENT: Tourism Development and Investment Company
of Abu Dhabi (TDIC), Solomon R. Guggenheim Foundation
COST: not disclosed
PRINCIPAL ARCHITECTS: Pei-Zhu, Tong Wu
DESIGN TEAM: Frisly Colop-Morales, He Fan, Yang Chao, Xue Dong

This pavilion by one of the rising stars of contemporary Chinese architecture is intended to fit closely with its surroundings, despite its design vocabulary. As the architect states, "While the dynamic, sculptural language of the building highlights its identity as a cultural landmark, distinguishing it from the adjacent commercial and residential buildings, the form of the pavilion reflects its function as a bridge between this urban fabric and the canal." The main exhibition hall will be a vast open space interrupted only by two angled cores that penetrate the building. An open sculptural stairway leads into this space from the public area below. Glazing is reduced to its minimum levels for reasons of the local climate, but a single large window on the south does offer views to the Biennale Park, in which the pavilion is situated. A ramp brings visitors down from the exhibition space to a ground-level café. Below the pavilion, a basement level will contain offices, flexible studio spaces/classrooms, retail space, and services.

Der Pavillon von Pei-Zhu, einem der aufsteigenden Sterne am chinesischen Architekturhimmel, soll sich trotz des gewählten architektonischen Vokabulars gut in seine Umgebung einpassen. Der Architekt erklärt: »Während die dynamische, skulpturale Sprache des Pavillons seine Identität als kulturelles Wahrzeichen betont und es von den Geschäfts- und Wohngebäuden in der Umgebung unterscheidet, spiegelt die Form seine Funktion als Mittler zwischen der städtischen Umgebung und dem Kanal wider.« Die Hauptausstellungshalle ist ein riesiger offener Raum, der nur von zwei schräg stehenden Gebäudekernen unterbrochen wird. Eine skulptural geformte Außentreppe führt von der öffentlichen Plaza in den darüberliegenden Ausstellungsraum. Aufgrund des Klimas wurden verglaste Flächen auf ein Minimum reduziert. Gleichwohl bietet auf der Südseite ein großes Fenster einen Ausblick auf den Biennale-Park, in dem sich der Pavillon befindet. Über eine Rampe gelangen die Besucher vom Ausstellungsbereich zu dem Café auf Erdgeschossniveau. Im Untergeschoss sind Büroräume, flexible Atelier- und Unterrichtsräume, eine Verkaufsfläche und Nebenräume untergebracht.

Ce pavillon proposé par l'une des étoiles montantes de l'architecture contemporaine chinoise devrait être bien adapté à son environnement en dépit du vocabulaire architectural choisi. L'architecte déclare que « si le langage structurel dynamique du bâtiment met en exergue son identité de monument culturel et se distingue des bâtiments résidentiels ou commerciaux qui l'entourent, la forme du pavillon reflète aussi sa fonction de point de rencontre entre le tissu urbain et le canal ». Le hall d'exposition principal sera constitué d'un grand volume ouvert uniquement interrompu par deux noyaux inclinés qui pénètrent le bâtiment. Un escalier ouvert et sculptural conduit à cet espace à partir de la zone d'accueil du public. Les ouvertures vitrées sont réduites au minimum pour s'adapter au climat local, mais une vaste ouverture au sud offre une vue sur le parc de la Biennale, dans lequel se trouve le pavillon. Une rampe conduit les visiteurs de l'espace d'exposition au café en rez-de-chaussée. Sous le pavillon, le niveau en sous-sol contiendra des bureaux, des ateliers/salles de cours, des magasins et les services techniques.

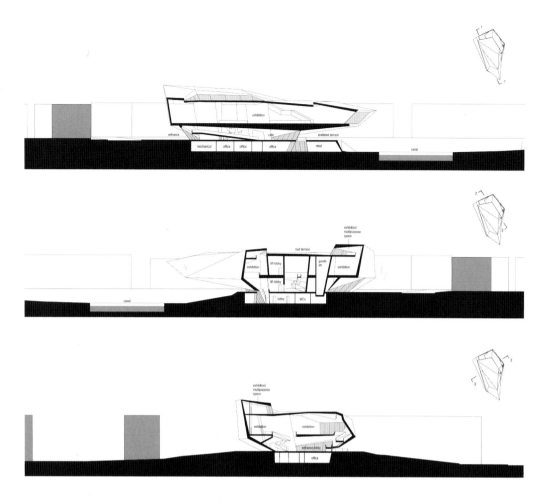

The angled and shifted floor design creates a dynamic impression as seen in these plans and elevations.

Die Dynamik des Gebäudes entsteht aus den schiefwinkligen, gegeneinander verschobenen Grundrissen und Schnitten.

Les niveaux inclinés et les décalages créent une impression dynamique perceptible sur les plans et les élévations.

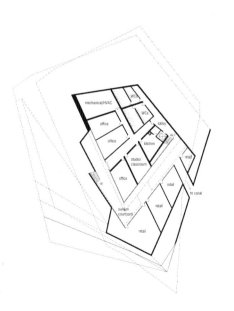

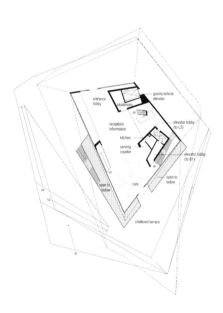

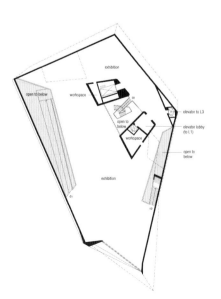

Interior views suggest a relatively complex but always linear space, with narrow openings bringing in natural light in this climate where clouds are relatively rare.

Die Innenraumperspektiven zeigen einen komplexen, aber linearen Raum. Weil in diesen Breitengraden nur selten Wolken am Himmel auftauchen, lassen die schmalen Öffnungen nur wenig Tageslicht in den Innenraum.

Les vues intérieures suggèrent un volume assez complexe, mais toujours linéaire. Les étroites ouvertures apportent la lumière naturelle dans un climat où les nuages sont relativement rares.

PHOTO CREDITS
IMPRINT

CREDITS PHOTOS / PLANS / DRAWINGS / CAD DOCUMENTS

To stay informed about upcoming TASCHEN titles, please request our magazine at www.taschen.com/magazine or write to TASCHEN, Hohenzollernring 53, D-50672 Cologne, Germany, contact@taschen.com, Fax: +49-221-254919. We will be happy to send you a free copy of our magazine which is filled with information about all of our books.

PROJECT MANAGEMENT: Florian Kobler and Mischa Gayring, Cologne
COLLABORATION: Katharina Krause, Cologne
PRODUCTION: Thomas Grell, Cologne
DESIGN: Sense/Net, Andy Disl and Birgit Reber, Cologne
GERMAN TRANSLATION: Caroline Behlen, Berlin
FRENCH TRANSLATION: Jacques Bosser, Paris

Printed in Italy
ISBN 978-3-8228-1396-6